Stacy Herzog Berk

EIMEAR LYNCH is a writer and editor who has worked at *Condé Nast Traveler*, *Town & Country*, and *Bloomberg Businessweek*. A five-time bridesmaid, she lives in Brooklyn.

HANYA YANAGIHARA lives in New York City.

THE
BRIDESMAIDS

True Tales of Love, Envy, Loyalty
...and Terrible Dresses

EIMEAR LYNCH

Series Editor HANYA YANAGIHARA

PICADOR ■ NEW YORK

www.picadorusa.com
www.twitter.com/picadorusa • www.facebook.com/picadorusa
picadorbookroom.tumblr.com

Picador® is a U.S. registered trademark and is used by St. Martin's Press under license from Pan Books Limited.

For book club information, please visit www.facebook.com/picadorbookclub or e-mail marketing@picadorusa.com.

Designed by Jonathan Bennett

Library of Congress Cataloging-in-Publication Data is available upon request.

ISBN 978-1-250-04177-7 (trade paperback)
ISBN 978-1-250-04178-4 (e-book)

Picador books may be purchased for educational, business, or promotional use. For information on bulk purchases, please contact Macmillan Corporate and Premium Sales Department at 1-800-221-7945, extension 5442, or write specialmarkets@macmillan.com.

First Edition: May 2014

10 9 8 7 6 5 4 3 2 1

This book is dedicated to the brides:
Stacy, Lily, Katelyn, Lauren, and Eileen

AUTHOR'S NOTE

Most of these stories are anonymous—meaning that names, locations, and other details have been changed.

CONTENTS

CONTENTS

CONTENTS

INTRODUCTION

The day after I got my book deal, my little sister's boyfriend told me he was going to propose. I immediately appointed myself maid of honor—I'm her only sister, after all—and did what any good bridesmaid would do: I whisked her out for an emergency manicure, subtly suggested more mascara before she left the house for her dinner date, and begged her boyfriend not to propose at the mall. I'd like to think that later that evening, after he got down on one knee in the Denver Botanic Gardens, she greatly appreciated how her glistening golden fingernails complemented her new diamond ring.

The result of all of this was that as I spent the next nine months interviewing almost eighty bridesmaids about the lovely, sentimental, and awful aspects of the role, I was also a bridesmaid myself. For the fifth time.

To be clear, I was cautiously excited. My previous turns in the role hadn't ruined me, but rather left me equal parts exhausted and intrigued. The first wedding I was in was a high school friend's, and I wore strapless pink chiffon. At five foot nine in four-inch heels, I think I was the tallest person there—and I spent the evening avoiding the dance invitations of a groomsman whose face lined up with my chest. Two weeks later, I stood up for another high school friend in a custom coral dress I actually loved, and I even did some helpful bridesmaidy things like stop her from crying about how beautiful the flowers were for the fourth time. Wedding number three was two months later, this time a college roommate's, and I wasn't looking my best: I had too-short bangs with a lopsided bob and a bitten-down manicure (which the other 'maids made me sneak out and remedy a few hours before the wedding). For the fourth, another college pal's, I wore strapless gray chiffon and finally had enough experience to know I would need longish hair, a pale-pink manicure, and not-too-tall heels in order to ensure optimal performance.

The bachelorette parties and weddings had taken me to Hilton Head, Charleston, Montauk, Vail, Santa Barbara, Chicago, Nashville, and Minneapolis in just two years. I loved reuniting with friends at all the parties, and I enjoyed standing up for each bride, but at times I didn't quite see the point of the role. Sure, I was a symbol of support, and, yes, it was great to get some actual face time with the brides, but I thought there must be more to being a bridesmaid—some secret girl things that I didn't understand.

And so I decided to write this book. But before I arrived at the meaning of bridesmaiding, I began worrying about my sister's big day. As I spoke to more and more 'maids, I realized that our scenario raised three important bridesmaid red flags:

1. I'm older than she is. When she got engaged, she was twenty-two to my twenty-six. Cue jealousy and/or stress about my unmarriedness.

2. Our styles differ. She wears polo shirts; I wear poofy skirts. Hello, bridesmaid dress fights!

3. It was my fifth tour of duty. Which could mean that I would be over it before it even began.

But soon, I saw that a fourth thing would be most integral to my experience: My sister was the ultimate bridesmaid-friendly bride. She said she didn't need a bridal shower; she asked that her bachelorette party be a dinner the Thursday before the wedding (as opposed to a weekend away); her bridesmaid dresses were flattering, simple, and only $100; and she chose a hotel for the reception so that there would be little fussing over details.

Basically, she wanted very little from me, which seemed glorious. But as the wedding neared, I started to hear the eighty bridesmaids I had interviewed collectively OMGing in my head—and I began feeling a little guilty about letting this milestone pass without much hullabaloo. Even if I think it can be a bit strange and dated to spend tons of time and money recognizing someone else's marriage, I realized that I would never have another chance to celebrate my sister in such an unabashed way.

That, to me, is one of the best parts about being a bridesmaid. It's a treat to be able to spoil sisters or dear friends who mean a lot to you. That is, *if* the celebrations are voluntary. As you'll see in this book, they often aren't.

This book is not about bridezillas (though there are a few). It's not about ugly dresses, either (though there are more than a few of those too). It's about the experience of being a bridesmaid— one of the rare things that many women have in common by the time they turn thirty. As I chatted with bridesmen, nemesisters, and even an astrologer, it was fascinating for me to hear how cultural traditions and social context make each bridesmaid's experience different. But it was also fantastic to see the similarities between those experiences: I never thought, for example, that I'd find the one commonality between a Burning Man regular and an ex-nun.

One thing every 'maid can agree on is that the role is an odd one. Questions abound: Why is it okay to make adult women wear matching dresses and shoes, and why do they carry flowers? What exactly are they supposed to be doing up there anyway? But there's also the flurry of emotions involved: By my calculations, 95 percent of bridesmaids bitch about the duty in the lead-up to a wedding, 75 percent tear up on the altar, and a full 100 percent feel at least a little bit flattered that they're BFF enough to score such top billing. No matter how disgruntled or annoyed she might seem, every bridesmaid experiences the high school smugness that comes with being part of the "in crowd." When a bridesmaid complains about all the weddings she's in, it is, at least in part, a humblebrag-y way of saying "I'm so popular."

Anyway, back to my sister. Although she asked very little of me—or maybe because she asked very little of me—I ended up really wanting to make her wedding special. I rounded up the other 'maids and we threw one hell of a bridal shower, with a whole table of pastel-colored desserts worthy of Marie Antoinette. I got sentimental, binding a photo book filled with quotes and notes from her friends. At her bachelorette party, I made sure everyone got drunk on margaritas sipped through penis-shaped straws. On her wedding morning, I went so far as to put on her deodorant for her. I blotted lipstick, train-fluffed, and bustled, and I even got a few laughs during my speech.

On the surface, these are the quintessential bridesmaid's duties, and you'll find them repeated throughout this book in various forms. But like many of the bridesmaids I interviewed, I found something much more meaningful about my sister's "wedding year" (to borrow a frightening term from "The Groom's Ex-Girlfriend," a story in this book): It brought us closer. We had an excuse to talk every week, and I got to know another side of her by spending time with her friends. It was also, in the words of "The Astrologer," a "marker point": a time of change when I couldn't help but reflect.

In fact, every bridesmaid I spoke to had interesting reflections about the role: Even the most embittered and bruised bridesmaids had carefully considered what the moment meant, and others had thoughts about bridesmaiding in the context of gender issues and societal mores. I was impressed by—and grateful for—the candor and self-awareness of the women (and occasional men) in this book.

So what did I learn from these chiffon-clad gals? Call me callous, but here's what you need to know in order to be a good, not-insane bridesmaid (if, that is, you make it past number 1).

1. Consider saying no. If you think your friend might have the Bridezilla gene, bow out before the bridal bonanza has begun. If you can't commit the money or time required, it pays to exit early; as the axed bridesmaids in this book will attest, you might lose your friendship if you stay on.

2. Don't give your opinion. A bride might say she wants it, but she doesn't. "I love it!" is all you ever need to say—especially about the bridesmaid dresses.

3. Be quiet. When stress runs high on the wedding day, the vibe should be positive but quiet. Loud talkers, I'm looking at you!

4. Take charge. There's nothing worse than being trapped on an e-mail chain with a bunch of brides-

maids masking passive aggression with *xoxo*s. Everyone will (eventually) thank you for choosing a bachelorette idea and nailing down the price and details.

5. Make friends. Yes, inter-bridesmaid alliances will help you get your way in stalemates over bachelorette venues and shower gifts, but that's not all: One of the best things about bridesmaiding is that it's a time to meet bridesmaids and groomsmen (and wedding laypeople, I guess) who could be future friends, coworkers, or boyfriends.

That last one's my favorite. When I wonder what I have to show for the five one-time-use dresses hanging in my closet, I think of the friendships I've made—or revived—during my two-year (and counting) career as a bridesmaid. These years of showers, bachelorette parties, bridal brunches, and weddings have brought me closer to old pals (brides included) and helped me forge new relationships. In fact, those friendships are so cemented that I think I could have a great crew of bridesmaids myself. But although I loved bridesmaiding for all of my friends—and I had a great time compiling the tales contained in this book—by the end of the project, I had come to a firm decision: My own future wedding will be a bridesmaid-free affair. Sorry, sis.

THE BRIDESMAIDS

THE MEDDLER

WHEN MY BEST FRIEND, Carrie, called me to tell me she was engaged—and to ask me to be her maid of honor—my response was, "Wait, you're dating someone?" I was so surprised: We had known each other since we were nine, and we had even gone to college together—and yet I didn't know that she had fallen in love? We were living in different cities at the time, and she had reconnected with another friend from childhood, Brandon, a few months earlier. They had been dating for four months when he presented her with an enormous diamond ring.

I was happy for her. But the thing is, there were rumors about Brandon. Everyone knew that he had hooked up with guys, and he had also apparently dated a guy for a whole summer during college. Carrie had heard the rumors, but she had also just turned thirty. And if you're single and thirty in Kentucky, you're basically an old maid.

When I saw them together, it was always a little off. He was either way too affectionate or way too distant, and gradually it emerged that they would get in these massive fights about strange things he was doing: He had lied about his savings accounts, he wouldn't come home some nights, and he convinced her to move in with him even though she was Christian and didn't want to live with a man until she was married. He made a show of saying grace when they ate out with friends, but when they were in bed together, he wanted to do really kinky stuff or nothing at all. Plus, he bought a red Volkswagen Beetle. What kind of guy buys a red Beetle?

Ever since we were teenagers, Carrie was the sort of girl who couldn't wait to get married and have kids. But when it was finally time to plan her wedding, she couldn't make any decisions. She was constantly crying, and she got to the point where she couldn't choose the bridesmaid dresses or even when or where to get married. When she finally set a date, she went into zombie mode: She bought a dress and picked out invitations, but she was constantly mopey. It was like he was chipping away at her soul.

At some point I realized that she thought it was scarier to call off the engagement than it would be to just marry him. She was terrified of embarrassment, and she couldn't see the difference between wanting to have a family and wanting to be in love with the right person. My gut was telling me it wasn't okay, so I called her parents. Her mom said, "Thank God, we don't think it's right either—she's going to be unhappy for the rest of her life." They had already sunk tens of thousands of dollars into the wedding, but they said they knew it was a bad idea all along. They were just too afraid to speak up. The invitations were about to go out, so we made a plan: I would go see Carrie the next weekend under the pretense of coming to help with wedding stuff.

Instead, I told her that I couldn't support the marriage. When I explained why I thought it was a mistake, she started crying. Then she went totally silent for two hours. When she finally started speaking again, she was still shaking and crying, but she seemed almost relieved. I had made the decision for her. "Okay," she said. "The wedding is off."

Carrie was mostly concerned about the practical things: What would happen to the million-dollar house they had bought? What would people think in our small, Christian hometown? Brandon was away for the weekend, so she called him and told him she was leaving. By now, her parents had arrived, and when she hung up, we were all like, "Keep the ring! It's not a family heirloom!" But she left it on the kitchen table.

I'll admit to having a high opinion of myself, but does that mean I think I have the right to tell people they shouldn't get married? I could have been making a huge mistake, and I was scared to death that she wouldn't find someone else. I hadn't met my husband yet either, and people certainly said that since I was miserable, I wanted Carrie to be miserable too. But I knew she'd be better off alone than with Brandon. And now, three years later, I think I was right: She just got married to an amazing guy who is absolutely perfect for her. And just four months after the breakup, Brandon used Carrie's ring to propose to a girl who looked exactly like her. They have kids now, according to Facebook. But yes, the rumors remain.

—K, 31

THE CRISIS MANAGER

THE DAY BEFORE MY SISTER KELLY'S WEDDING, there was a forecast for storms. The ceremony was to be held outdoors, at a farm in rural Wisconsin, so we decided at the last minute that we'd need to rent a tent. It was sunny for the pictures, and then the skies opened up just as the ceremony was about to start. It was really romantic, standing in the little tent with rain coming down all around us. And the sky was blue by the time we left the tent for the cocktail hour, so we thought things had worked out great.

The reception was in a pavilion with a tin roof and walls. I couldn't tell you when it started raining again—I was organizing speeches, playing videos, putting on music—but I remember when I started getting alarmed: when I saw about an inch of water collecting in the corner of the dance floor. I stopped dancing and pulled out my phone. A tornado was predicted to touch down within an hour or two, and within a few miles of us. You couldn't hear how loud the wind was howling over the music, but when I peeked outside, it was ugly. I rounded up a few friends with good phone service and asked them to keep my sister out of the loop at all costs—but to stay on top of the weather report.

It was like a Sandra Bullock movie: The tornado was just a few miles away from a room containing everyone I loved. I pulled the best man aside and we discussed whether we needed to evacuate. We knew there was a house on the grounds, but it was locked, so we considered breaking a window and getting everyone into the basement. Then we lost power. I had been telling my sister that it was just a storm, but we had to tell her at that point that it was a tornado. She was remarkably calm. I was ridiculously stressed out.

I thought that when the power went out everyone would want to leave, but the bar was still there and there was room for dancing. We were stuck, so people just partied harder. The big stroke of luck was that Kelly had wanted the reception to be candlelit, so we had lots of lanterns and candles on the tables. People just hung out, avoiding the corner of the venue that was slowly filling up with water. There was no music, but at one point my stepsiblings—who are the loudest people ever, and have beautiful voices—were posted in a corner singing, with people joining in. The caterers made an Irish exit at some point, leaving all the dirty dishes on the tables.

I alternated between running around looking for a generator and frantically checking my phone to track the tornado as it worked its way toward us. I wondered whether we should shut the wedding down. We ushered some families with young kids into a more permanent structure—a big barn—so they would feel safer. But by the time we had done that, all of the weather-checking iPhone users had determined that the tornado was at last moving away from us. It wasn't going to get any worse. We were safe.

And we were also covered in mud. The whole venue had turned into a mud pit, so that by the time we got into town at the end of the night, my sister's dress was brown from the knees down, and I looked like I had been wrestling in pudding. All of our shoes were done for, and my boyfriend's slacks were so dredged in mud that he had to throw them away the next day.

But the wedding was awesome. People still tell me it was the best party ever. It must have been something about celebrating survival and being trapped with such good people. I have to say, the whole experience gave me a greater appreciation for my sister. When I saw her drinking a beer at a dive bar in a gorgeous dress that was black with mud, I was pretty impressed. And of course there were the inevitable jokes about bad weather predicting a good marriage: If a thunderstorm is good luck on a wedding day, then a tornado had to be excellent, right?

—T, 27

THE TIMEKEEPER

MY BEST FRIEND, Katie, is horrendously, always, 100 percent of the time, perpetually late for everything. She's famous for it. She's not a bad person, but she really believes that she can get from where she is to wherever she needs to be in ten minutes.

I, on the other hand, think of myself as a timekeeper. At my own wedding, when the clock struck the appointed hour, I was like, "Okay, let's go NOW," even though people were still filing into the church. Katie was a bridesmaid in my wedding, and I made her spend the night with me in the bridal suite so I could make sure she wouldn't be late. I guess it's odd that we're friends, but we've both been this way since we met in sixth grade.

Part of the problem with Katie is that she has this fantastically beautiful chestnut hair. It's wavy and bouncy and perfect, but it requires styling. My hair is as flat as a pancake, and I know nothing about girly stuff, but I am an expert in Katie's hair timetable. If I am going to an event with Katie, I show up at her house about three hours before we're supposed to meet. I say, "What's the plan? Are you wearing it curly or flat? Because if you're wearing it curly you need to be putting in product now, and if you're flat-ironing it, shouldn't you have plugged in your straightener already?" Basically I just insert myself into her hygiene, which is kind of crazy. It's not like she's totally vain or even insistent on being perfectly groomed—she's just so easily distracted.

But at a wedding, with vendors, stress, old people, and hoopla, tardiness just wasn't an option. My only job as Katie's maid of honor was to get her to places on time. But it wasn't going to be easy. I had a newborn and a three-year-old, and I was a basket case. I have all these strategies for getting her where she needs to be—I'm obsessive about it—and my poor husband bore the brunt of my madness. He didn't begrudge the showers, the bachelorette party, or the intense planning, but he did suggest that I was treating him like a slave. Boys have less patience for that sort of stuff.

I had a ton of stuff to schlep from our home in San Francisco to the wedding, which was in Napa: There were multiple bridesmaid dresses, enough baby things for a three-day weekend, and a bunch of gifts. On the day we were set to leave, my husband comes walking out of the house and says he's ready to go. He's clutching a few clothes in his hand like you would hold laundry, and he has a dry-cleaning bag over his shoulder. I couldn't take it. I seem to remember saying, "Are you serious? Can you fucking pack a bag? Look at all this stuff and tell me why you can't put your fucking clothes in a bag." I might have been on edge.

We didn't speak on the drive to Napa, and when we got to the hotel, I stepped out of the car and fell into a trench—the place was undergoing some sort of construction. As I lay in the ditch, clutching a foot that I would soon discover was broken, my husband stood over me laughing. He was still mad, and I still had my eye on the prize. "Don't tell anyone!" I hissed. The show had to go on.

I hobbled through the hotel to determine what the greatest distraction would be on the big day. It was easy to find: Surely everyone would congregate at the beautiful, central pool, and it'd be hard to lure Katie away from that scene and into the bridal suite. I approximated the getting-ready time and added a few hours for good measure, and the next day I started corralling her away from the pool about six hours before the ceremony was set to begin. Once I had her sitting inside, I kept the whole hair-and-makeup routine relatively focused and I found a single image to hammer into her mind: that of her fiancé's ninety-year-old grandmother teetering in her little heels until Katie appeared. It became my continual refrain.

By the time she walked down the aisle, I think she was thoroughly annoyed. But Katie picked me to be her maid of honor—she knows how I am! And after years of plotting, strategizing, and forcing Katie into semipunctuality, I felt ridiculously accomplished when her wedding started only thirty minutes behind schedule. Which isn't to say I didn't suffer: It took a good three days to make up with my husband, and to this day, whenever the weather turns shitty or I get into certain yoga positions, that ache in my left foot is a reminder of Katie's wedding day.

—L, 40

THE DAUGHTER

I DIDN'T MEET MY MOM'S HUSBAND until after they got engaged. That's because of a rule I set in place when I was thirteen: I told my mom that I was happy for her, no matter whom she dated, but that I didn't want to meet any boyfriends unless the relationship was serious. My parents got divorced when I was eleven, and by age thirteen, I knew it would be confusing for me to get to know every guy she went out with. Then my dad passed away when I was sixteen.

Since then, my mom has dated a lot. I never liked how certain guys treated her. People say so much through their tone of voice, and there were guys who slowly, subtly belittled her to the point of making her unsure of her whole self-worth. She had dated one guy on and off for a long time, but eventually she just woke up and said, "What the hell am I doing?" She was in therapy, and she finally said, "Fuck it. This isn't how I want to live my life." She dumped the guy and went to a friend's party, and that's where she met Harry. She had always dated tall, dark, handsome Italian guys, and here was Harry, who is shorter than she, with a shock of white hair. It's like as soon as she realized she was in a pattern that was making her unhappy, she broke it. It worked out well.

When Harry came along, my mom was forty-nine. She finally got it. She was happy. I don't know if she got it and then she met Harry, or she got it because of him—but when she called me to tell me she was engaged, she was over the moon. At that point I had heard so many wonderful things about Harry, and whenever she told stories about him, she couldn't stop laughing. They had dated for only a few months, but she explained to me that you know really quickly when someone is right for you by the time you reach a certain age—that you don't waste any time with the dating crap and angsty stuff that younger people worry about.

Harry proposed on Halloween, and I met him for the first time on Christmas. I was worried it would be awkward, especially because he had two sons and my mom had me and my sister: I was twenty-four and living in a nearby city, but my sister was sixteen and still at home. But everything clicked; all our personalities matched well. What I remember most is that Harry sought my mom's opinion on things. Not necessarily on carpet colors or cereal preference, but about important issues of the day: He'd ask her what she thought about things he had read about in the newspaper. And when I'd leave the room for a minute, they'd be laughing like maniacs when I returned. Harry has his quirks—he's stingy about certain things, and he pulls some boneheaded moves—but he was so, so tolerant of all the ridiculousness that came along with my mom: her teenage daughter, the two dogs and two cats, and most of all, her own general looniness.

That looniness played out when it came to planning the wedding. It's cynical to say that being a bridesmaid is a thankless job, but you have to recognize that even the most beloved friend, sister, or mother will eventually flip the crazy switch. My mom wanted a no-fuss, quiet, backyard wedding, and she asked me to arrange everything for her. She wanted it to be the opposite of her first wedding, which was a huge church ceremony with a fancy reception at the country club where my mom and dad met in golf lessons when they were thirteen. Her mantra during the planning process was, "I don't care! Do whatever. I don't care!" So I took charge—ordering flowers, setting up the caterer, coordinating everything. Then, three weeks before the ceremony, she decided *she* wanted to be in charge, and she spent the next few days rabidly changing most of my orders and bookings.

I have no idea where this comes from. I guess a bride wants her day to be perfect, and what she envisions—even if she claims she doesn't have any idea what she wants. It's so weird how people get, but you just have to grit your teeth and say, "This will be over soon." And it was, and the day itself was lovely. Of course, our loud, boisterous relatives descended and began fighting over issues that had been festering since childhood. And my sister had all the attitude that comes along with being sixteen and suddenly having to share a bathroom with a boy. But our new family—including Harry and his sons—presented a small united front against our larger family and all its drama. We knew what my mom wanted, and we assuaged each familial spat so she wouldn't have to.

I'm still learning from the wedding, which was two years ago. It reminded me to be patient with my family and with myself. I learned that I'm looking for someone who is good to me, and good to my family, above everything else. I'd love to be able to do what my mom did and look through my ex-boyfriends and find a commonality that I could avoid. But I honestly can't see anything mine have in common—except for the fact that they were all wrong. And in terms of getting to where she is, I can only hope it happens before I'm forty-nine.

—M, 27

THE ACCIDENTAL AMERICAN
BRIDESMAID IN ITALY

MY FRIENDS LEAH AND LUCA met in a gay bar in San Francisco. He's a handsome Italian guy who said, "Hey, *bellisima*," and it turned out they were both straight. They're not your typical couple, and his family is wonderfully atypical too: His mom, Giovanna, is a fun, vivacious woman who barely speaks English and dates a strapping gardener named Mario, who's twenty-five years her junior.

I wasn't officially in the wedding party, but I became a de facto bridesmaid as the weekend unfolded. Leah and Luca's wedding was at his family's beautiful, sprawling 150-year-old house in a picture-perfect town in the Italian mountains. It was all green vistas—a total dream. When my husband and I arrived in town, Mario took us to what he said was the first Irish pub in Italy: Murphy's. I cannot stress enough that this is the cutest, tiniest Italian village you've ever seen, one of those places where everyone knows everyone else. So he ran into a friend, they started talking in Italian, and all of a sudden they jumped up and Mario said, "I want to show you something." It was a really dark, moonless night, and he took us down a dirt road toward the middle of nowhere. We totally trusted Mario, but there was a language barrier, and I started wondering whether we were going to be involved in some borderline-illegal activity. Like, I've never even smoked pot! And then we arrived at these greenhouses. My heart was really pounding until Mario flipped on all the lights to reveal big potted plants. Which were apparently for the wedding, so we started helping him pick the best ones. And all of this was being done at 11:00 P.M. two nights before the big event. After that, I knew it wouldn't be like any American wedding I had ever seen.

My husband and I arrived too late to partake in the bachelor and bachelorette parties. They stayed out all night and returned to the house, hungover and exhausted, the day before the wedding. They went to bed around 7:00 A.M., just as Mario got up and started mowing the lawn and getting supplies together for the decorations. As the only other people awake, my husband and I were handed rolls of tulle that Leah wanted to be draped across a huge expanse of yard. No one gave us directions, so we started rigging things to the roof and climbing trees with bunches of tulle in our arms.

Leah had ordered a wedding dress via a made-in-China "designer gown" Web site, and when it arrived three weeks before the wedding, it was a total disaster. So she went out and bought a ream of satin and had been sewing it on her body for the past week. It was far from complete, so the whole goal the day before the wedding was to finish the friggin' dress. At some point when my husband and I were still trying to figure out the tulle situation, I went to ask her what it should look like. I found her surrounded by friends who were literally sewing satin onto her body. She was totally calm and said, "You'll make it beautiful. I trust you." And that's when I realized I was running this show.

We kept draping the tulle from the trees and the roof, so that it was suspended over the gigantic yard, and I crafted this huge tulle poof ball for the apex. I made paper-heart garlands and strung them around the place, too, and figured out where the altar would be before arranging the mismatchy chairs for guests. That's when I discovered that they weren't planning on rehearsing. That wouldn't do. Once I lined everyone up, Luca turned to my husband and said, "Oh yeah, you're going to officiate." Ha! They had an Italian officiant, but they also wanted everything in English. So Luca spent a few hours trying to explain, in English, the meaning of romantic Italian poems, which was adorable.

The wedding day arrived, and Leah was still being sewn into her dress. She had forgotten to get bouquets for her bridesmaids, so she told me to go to the neighbor's garden and snip off a few hydrangeas. This was really nerve-wracking for me, because I'm the lamest rule-following person there ever was, but I snuck up to these crazy beautiful hydrangea bushes anyway and started cutting. The neighbor came out. She spoke really quickly in Italian, and I'm like, "Ahhh, wedding! Wedding!" and she nodded and went back inside. Somehow, I found ribbon and fashioned four little bouquets. My next task involved tramping around the house and gardens in search of the ring-bearer, who was engaged in his own version of hide-and-seek.

Even though she was essentially wearing a toga, Leah looked absolutely gorgeous. The ceremony was a riot because it was technically translated into English, even though everything seemed funnier and longer in Italian. When the Italian officiant said, "Speak now, or forever hold your peace," three girls came running down the aisle screaming. I guess it's some sort of tradition, but none of us Americans got it at all because we hadn't heard the English translation yet.

The food was totally amazing. While I had been fastening tulle sheets to trees and shingles and Leah was being sewn into her dress, Giovanna had been cooking pastas, pork loins, Italian sausages, and delicious mini-cakes. We danced on the lawn and paused for gelato at two in the morning. It really could have been a romantic comedy. In fact, one of the tall, blond bridesmaids—a Floridian—hooked up with an Italian guy who was unbelievably gorgeous, but only five foot three. It was too good to be true, and when they dated for a little while afterward we all hoped they'd be the next couple down the aisle—I'm sure I could've gotten a gig as their wedding planner, after all.

—I, 28

THE BRIDESMAID-OFFICIANT

MY FRIEND MELANIE TOLD ME that she wanted to propose to her girlfriend, Emily, at about the same time that Emily told me she wanted to propose to Mel. They were having trouble figuring out their roles in this particular instance—they didn't know who should propose. They both wanted to commit, but each was confused as to why the other hadn't taken the next step.

They both bought rings. Melanie had planned a huge, beautiful engagement involving a camping trip and a hot-air balloon, and Emily thought Mel was dragging her feet. She kept asking me whether she should propose, and I didn't want to say yes because I knew Mel had planned something—but I didn't want to say no, either, because I didn't want to ruin the surprise. It was funny—they were getting so mad at each other! In the end, Emily got upset and proposed out of frustration, and Mel did the big proposal even though they were already engaged.

Immediately afterward, they asked me to officiate the wedding. I'm a lawyer, and they thought I would be comfortable speaking in front of a lot of people. They also asked if I'd help with the planning process, so I had a hybrid role as a bridesmaid-officiant. The wedding was going to be in Georgia, where same-sex marriage isn't recognized, so it was more of a ceremonial thing. Mel is a strong, Southern woman, and her big Baptist family is incredibly supportive of both her and Emily. Emily's dad isn't as accepting, so they assumed that he wouldn't be there.

I wore a pink dress they picked out for me. They looked at so many dresses, and this was the second one I'd bought. Emily is the more feminine of the two, and she fell head over heels in love with this dress. It was just a little A-line thing. Emily wore a traditional wedding dress, and Mel wore white slacks, a white shirt, and a pink-and-white vest. I think if she could do it again, she'd wear a wedding dress—she has become much more feminine in the past few years. My mom made a collar and leash that their dog wore in the audience.

There was tension over who I'd spend the day with. Emily wanted me to keep her calm and to help arrange things, but Mel wanted me with her too. In the end, I spent a few hours with Mel doing the usual bride stuff—hair and nails—and I got dressed with Emily. And I spent the time in between running around like a headless chicken dealing with last-minute wedding stuff.

Speaking of last-minute, Emily's dad showed up at the eleventh hour. Everyone was shocked—he fought the union with such vigor that she almost didn't even send him an invite. She had come to terms with their relationship, so it was more stressful than anything when he showed up. A bundle of nerves and agitation, he walked so fast that he practically dragged Emily down the aisle. It was a nice gesture, but he left almost immediately after the ceremony.

The girls had given me parts they wanted to include in the ceremony, and I wrote a lot of stuff myself. But I ended up cutting it down because I wanted it to be about what they had to say to each other. My main message was one of support. Their new life wouldn't be easy, but the entire congregation would all be there to offer help or reassurance whenever times got tough. I was speaking about the general ups and downs of marriage, but also the prejudice they would undoubtedly face: After all, they were married in the South just a few months after North Carolina passed an amendment making same-sex marriage unconstitutional. That ruling weighed heavily on them, even though they didn't live there, so I wanted to make sure they felt supported by the people who mattered.

The reception was in an old barn. It was relaxed and fun, with dancing, cake, and toasts, just like many of the straight weddings I've attended. The girls could have thought outside the box, I guess, but they didn't want to be seen as different. They just wanted to be together.

—S, 29

THE VERY PREGNANT OBGYN

I WAS CONVINCED I was infertile until October of 2009. I've always had this pathology where I think I'm experiencing all the problems my patients have, but when I found out I was pregnant, I obviously realized that I was mistaken—and I became convinced that my baby would have some sort of abnormality. This was my horror—that I'd have a baby without a brain or something—so I was really concerned about bringing home a live baby that would turn into a human being.

I was less concerned about being an eight-months-pregnant bridesmaid in my friend Jamie's wedding. At first, I was a little nervous. Jamie is also an OBGYN, and she's a super-duper planner. Right after I found out I was pregnant, she sent around an e-mail asking her bridesmaids for their dress sizes. So even though I tell my patients to keep their pregnancies secret until the second trimester—this is in case they miscarry, or anything goes wrong—I had to tell Jamie much earlier: I didn't know what style would fit me because I didn't know what I'd look like by the wedding. She was so happy for me that it made me even more excited to be a part of her big day.

It turns out I wasn't alone. Of the four OBGYN bridesmaids in the wedding, two ended up being pregnant; another, Mia, was two months postpartum on the wedding day. You can imagine how much fun we were. As you might guess, the bachelorette party was a pretty sober affair. We went to dinner and to a cabaret, but we were old ladies by then anyway. It was nothing like the bachelorette parties of my twenties—and I mean *nothing*. But Jamie was amazingly supportive. I guess because she's used to dealing with pregnant people.

My biggest concern was the dress. None of us could accurately guess how big we'd be at the wedding. At one point I asked if I could wear a shower curtain. I am normally a size six, but I ordered a size twenty because I was so worried that the dress would be too small. Mia ordered a big size, too, because she wasn't sure how big she'd be after the baby came. You would think I'd be worried about traveling—it was a destination wedding, in the Bahamas—but by that point in my pregnancy, most of my fears had been allayed; my doctor friends had convinced me that I was carrying a healthy child. I also felt like I was in pretty good hands. If I delivered at the wedding, I'd be okay. I was literally surrounded by obstetricians. The bride herself could deliver me if things got really dire.

My dress, which was mint green and satin, needed massive alterations. It had a tank top and an empire waist, and then the huge curtain over my belly. It wasn't attractive; I sent it to Goodwill the second I got home. The other pregnant bridesmaid wasn't as pregnant as I was, and she chose more of a V-neckline. She looked great.

The wedding ended up being a really relaxing conclusion to my pregnancy—all the sun and sand and good friends. There we were, a bunch of pregnant ladies hopping around on the dance floor, and Mia with her two-month-old baby. If we've ever looked like OBGYNs, it was then. I did have that huge feeling because none of my clothes fit—even my fat clothes—but I wasn't unhealthy: I was just *that* pregnant. Now, when I look at the pictures, I'm no longer embarrassed by my big belly in the green dress. I'm happy I can show my daughter that she was at Jamie's wedding too.

—J, 30

THE (ALMOST) EX-FRIEND

WHEN I WAS IN MY LATE TWENTIES, I worked with a woman from Germany named Anja. I expected to dislike her. I went to college with a German student who was very stern and aggressive, so I thought she'd be the same way. But in reality, she was spontaneous and flexible and friendly, and much more open than I am. She became my best friend, and I was sad to say good-bye to her when she moved back to Hamburg a year after we met.

We stayed in touch until she got busy at work, and I became the only one calling or initiating e-mail contact. It would take longer and longer for her to reply—and even longer when she had her son. When she had her second son, she practically disappeared. It felt like our friendship was over.

At first I was upset. I didn't grow up with billions of friends, so I really cherish the ones I have. I yelled at her and guilted her. I couldn't accept the loss of our friendship. And then, eventually, I stopped caring. But for some reason, Anja still cared. Three times a year, she would send a sincere e-mail apologizing for her absence. But seven years after she left, that just about ended. By then I had accepted the fact that our friendship had run its course.

After a year of silence, I got an e-mail from Anja six weeks before Christmas. I was shocked to see that it was an invitation to her wedding—which was taking place a month later. I had no plans to go to Germany around Christmas for someone I no longer talked to, but I wasn't brave enough to say that. So I said nothing. After a week or so, she sent another e-mail. I continued my reply of no reply. A week later, I got a long, heartfelt letter explaining why I had to attend the wedding. I was always encouraging her to marry Lars, and because I had so much confidence in their relationship, she wanted me to be her *trauzeugin,* the German version of the bridesmaid.

There's not a big marriage culture in Germany: Many people get married years after they have children, like Anja and Lars did. Anja wrote that she was much more nervous about getting married than she had been about having kids. She said she wanted me there for comfort, that I was one of the only people who thought she should bother with marriage. I bought a ticket to Hamburg.

What are bachelorette parties like in Germany? Well, custom dictates that the bride dress up like a sexy Minnie Mouse, with a veil on, and sell small bottles of alcohol on the street. Needless to say, we didn't have a bachelorette party. She had two kids for goodness' sake! Instead, on the day before the wedding, we went to a vintage store around the corner from her house. She bought a funky leather skirt, and she wore it the next day when we set off to the *standesamt,* or registrar's office. German law requires couples to be married by a government official, and since I was a witness, I had to present my passport and sign several papers. Everything was so formal: The bride and groom, the bridesmaid and groomsman, and an official translator all sat at a table in front of this serious German civil servant. The guests sat quietly behind us.

Afterward, we went to lunch at a little Italian restaurant. There were no toasts, there was no American-style wedding cake. Just platters of family-style food, wine, and a few hours of talking and laughing. Later on, everyone went to a tequila bar. I knew most of the people there, but not well, and I felt a little guilty: I didn't speak German, and I had displaced all of Anja's oldest friends to be her maid of honor. Plus everyone was paired off, and I was single. I tried talking to the groomsman, Sebastian, who I had discerned was also single, but he was monosyllabic. He spent most of his time chain-smoking cigarettes and drinking. Anja's parents had made him promise to walk me to her apartment at the end of the night, but by then he was so drunk that I was the one walking him home.

The next day, Anja and Lars brought Sebastian and me to a Christmas market in Cologne. Sebastian and I ended up alone, and we started talking about potato salad. It was funny; he was interesting. I was shocked that he was so nice. When we went back to Anja's at the end of the night, we sat on the couch while I obsessively searched for *30 Rock* episodes online. He put his hand on my knee, and we kissed. We shared a bed that night, but nothing happened. I left for the airport the next morning.

When I got back to New York, there was an e-mail from Sebastian in my in-box. From then on, we wrote each other a lot—probably five thousand e-mails in just a few months. I'd call him when I woke up every morning, and we'd talk for three or four hours on Friday nights. I'm neither flexible nor spontaneous, but for some reason I thought this was going to be something special. I'd never really had boyfriends because I would rather be alone than with someone stupid; I personally coined the phrase "This isn't going to work out." But this time it was right—with Sebastian, I felt comfortable and relaxed.

Within seven months of Anja's wedding, Sebastian and I were married at Manhattan's City Hall. I decided to move to Germany, and we have a good life here. We live in a smallish city in northern

Germany, and since I'm a big-city gal, it seems romantic. I teach English and write, and things with Sebastian are good. People say your first year of marriage is the most difficult, but ours was easy. I'm loud and he's quiet; he's reserved while I'm easily excited. And I owe my happiness, in a way, to Anja. I found my husband because I didn't let my anger and frustration stop me from experiencing the joy of supporting my friend.

—M, 42

THE BRIDESMAN

MICHELLE WAS AN UNUSUAL PERSON and a wonderful writer. We met when she was a junior in college, and she was this introverted woman who was slowly pushing herself to move beyond her shyness. We went to a small liberal arts school, and I met her at a dance one night in the all-purpose room. She tapped me on the shoulder and told me we had a class together. Did I want to dance? Later on, she told me that I was the only guy she had ever asked.

She sensed that we had things in common, and she was right. She and I became great friends, along with another guy named Sean, and the three of us did everything together: We went to performances and art shows, we worked in the theater department. This was 1985. After college, she went to grad school and met a crazy, hard-driving, high-energy writer who worked with kids in poor neighborhoods in Detroit. He drove Michelle forward—they had a wonderful relationship and an unusual life. They both had master's degrees, but they took itinerant teaching jobs and chose to live with very little money. She wrote and gardened. He would lecture at a well-known college for a few months, and then leave to work in an auto shop for part of the year. And then he proposed.

She never asked Sean and me to be in the wedding. As the date approached, she just said, "And you guys will be up there with me when we get married" when she was explaining the logistics. She didn't think it was a question that needed to be asked. She had female friends from college and grad school who might have been better for the job, so it was surprising and wonderful to be chosen to be her "bridesmen."

The wedding was in a field not far from where they lived in rural Ohio. At a certain hour on the appointed day—maybe around 1:00 P.M.—people came to their little house and asked whether it was time for the wedding. Michelle said they were waiting a bit. It wasn't because they were nervous or having second thoughts; they just lived on their own schedule. Part of it might have had to do with the fact that she had been diagnosed with non-Hodgkin's lymphoma a few months before their wedding. She was twenty-six, and although the initial diagnosis was not life-threatening, it affected her. She was living in a way that suited her because she probably believed, without saying it, that she didn't know how long her life would be.

But that day, when they were at last ready to go, we drove thirty minutes to a hundred-year-old farm, where there were a few chairs set out in a field next to a row of corn. A few older people sat in the chairs, and everyone else stood or sat on the edge of the lawn. Sean and I stood with Michelle; the groom's brother stood with him. I didn't think much of it—us standing there with her, as men—until it was time to exchange the rings and she handed me her bouquet. It felt funny and wonderful to hold it as they finished the very simple service. After they'd said their vows, we all hugged and the new couple walked forward into the crowd of their friends. The other bridesman blew bubbles. The reception was a potluck, with dishes set on tables in the field.

A month after the wedding, Michelle began chemotherapy

and radiation. She was a small person to start with, and she diminished very quickly and lost all of her hair. Her husband was this intense, caring, and empathetic person who believed that they could beat it, and beat it, and beat it away. He never stopped believing that as she went in and out of the hospital every other year. I had never met someone so young whose body had been so hammered by disease. But they kept going, with him driving on. Sean and I would visit her in the hospital, and as weak as she'd be, she'd always happily engage us in conversation about art and writing and theater. She'd get very ill, and then she'd come back. It was amazing. She was so tiny, but so strong.

After fourteen years, it finally wore her out. My wife and I were on vacation when Michelle died, and we drove twenty hours to make it to her wake on time. We picked up Sean, the other bridesman, on the way.

When Michelle was alive, I would have thought about her wedding and smiled. It was a tiny thing and a huge thing. It felt simple and sweet to be surrounded by people who loved her and her husband, and who appreciated their unconventionality. But in retrospect it was much larger than that. If she hadn't married him, I'm sure she wouldn't have lived half as long as she did. Their union kept her alive. Her husband drove the illness away for a long time with who he was, and with how he carried her.

—J, 48

THE WORLD RECORD SETTER

I HELPED SET THE GUINNESS WORLD RECORD for most bridesmaids in a wedding. There were 110 of us.

We set the record by accident. The proud owner of Jill's Tumble World here in Chesapeake, Ohio (population: 745), Jill, was marrying a coach at her gym. All her students wanted to be a part of the wedding, and even though there were a lot of them, she thought it was important not to leave anyone out.

Which is so Jill. She has a really warm personality. I met her because my daughter was in her class at the gym, and we just couldn't stop talking. We became walking buddies and that was it.

I was the maid of honor, but I didn't have to do much. Jill picked out long, strapless teal dresses for the adult bridal party—there were seven of us—and she posted an invitation to her students on the Tumble World Web site. She asked any potential bridesmaids to wear the wedding colors: white, purple, or teal. We threw a shower, and almost all of them made it: It was at the gym.

When we arrived at the church on the wedding day, there sure were a lot of people there. There were all these girls swarming around, wearing the colors. They ranged in age from three to seventeen, and each girl carried a single rose. The older girls helped the little ones get down the aisle. I just took care of Jill while another bridesmaid's mother formed a 110-person-long line. The students sat in the first few rows of the church, and the adult bridesmaids stood by the altar. It was surprisingly calm, with no drama or stress—and a lot of joy.

About two-thirds of our town (or more than 400 people) were at the wedding, so it was as great a spectacle as we've had here. The local news station was there, but I don't know who called them because Jill definitely didn't. She had no idea it'd be a big deal. The reception was really nice. It was out in the country, in tents by a barn. There was a DJ and the kids were so excited. Yes, there were some silly moves on the dance floor. Everyone had fun.

I guess Jill's dad counted up the bridesmaids, videotaped the whole thing, and then checked into the record. Once he filed to set the record, the story got picked up by the *Today* show, and folks talked about it around here for a while. It was one of the biggest things to happen in this town, and although Jill was happy about it, she wasn't obsessed or anything. She hasn't been watching to see if she'll be topped. She's very busy with the gymnastics, so I'm sure it's the furthest thing from her mind.

How many groomsmen were there? I don't remember—nobody pays attention to them! There were probably only seven, but the groom didn't feel outnumbered. He was so overjoyed after the ceremony that he did a back tuck right down the aisle.

—J, 39

THE PRISON BRIDESMAID

I HAD MY RESERVATIONS ABOUT MIKE. I hadn't spent a lot of time with him, and though I knew he and my sister had a strong bond, I was still apprehensive about the man. He is in prison, after all. When my sister told me they were getting married, it was hard to be 100 percent on board.

I was living overseas when Elise started dating Mike, and I've always been sad that I wasn't there at the beginning, before he was in prison. They lived in neighboring towns in rural Oklahoma, and met online. During that time, he was in and out of jail for various minor infractions. They'd date briefly and then he'd get arrested again. The thing is that incarceration is standard in these small towns. It was like a rite of passage in his family. It wasn't shocking to me that he had been arrested. Not at all.

Finally, he got nabbed for breaking parole, and he was sent to prison. They started writing letters again. They'd send these lovely, handwritten notes once or twice a day. When she told me they were involved, I immediately thought of how hard it is to break out of the prison cycle. But my sister is very determined, and she's wonderful at working through tough situations. I knew she'd be up for the challenge of this relationship.

My sister's a fixer. She left our little town to get a master's

degree in social work, with the goal of coming back to Oklahoma to change things. I'm introverted, but she has never shied
away from mediating an argument or asking a stranger what's
wrong. That was what concerned me when she started getting
serious with Mike. I thought she might just want to save him.

It was easy for me to understand what she did for him: She
helped him solve problems; she served as a counselor of sorts.
But it was harder for me to see what she got out of the relationship. I'm embarrassed to say that I didn't meet Mike until the month
after he proposed. I just never thought I'd be meeting my sister's
fiancé in a maximum-security prison.

The rules about visiting prison are very complicated. First
you have to fill out an application and pay for a background check.
Next there's a list of stuff you can't wear: no t-shirts with writing
on them, nothing low cut, no metal, no wire bra, no holes, no long
shirt underneath a shorter shirt, no turtlenecks. I was so scared I'd
mess it up for my sister, so I planned my outfit weeks in advance.
Before that first visit, we had to wake up at 4:00 A.M. to make it
before 8:00 A.M. We were questioned, we waited, we went through
a metal detector, we were patted down. We waited some more in
a holding area, we got stamps on our hands, and finally we saw
Mike in the visiting room.

From that first moment, I saw a spark in my sister—a happiness. My sister can be very serious, but here she was like a giggly
schoolgirl. Her guard was down. All my fear and anxiety disappeared in the heart of the prison—where they'd created this in-
fectious bubble of happiness that put me at ease. I saw that Mike
is a cheerleader and a planner when it comes to her: He supports
her plans to improve her diet and exercise habits; he helps her
stay motivated about work. They're open with each other, and
they seem to be committed to helping each other become better
people. Still, they had to stick to the rules. Mike and Elise could

kiss only once, for less than twenty seconds, and they could only hold hands on top of the table.

The planning began once Mike and Elise were engaged. He proposed to her over vending-machine Cheetos in the prison guest room—he still had four years left. She requested a few wedding dates, which were denied, and once she finally got approval she started looking for a dress. It had to be a certain length, with a certain amount of layers, and it couldn't show her shoulders. She e-mailed the chaplain photos of some of the contenders to make sure they were up to code. At last she found a gorgeous blue-and-black calf-length dress, which she paired with a black cardigan. She looked perfect. I didn't wear anything fabulous: just black pants and a dress shirt that would get me past security (and no jewelry—that's not allowed either).

Elise had to apply for approval for every object she wanted to bring. She had eight things: a camera, the two batteries in the camera, the pastor's Bible, the flowers, the ribbon around the flowers, and the two rings. She stalked the chaplain for months to organize everything and to secure approval to bring in our own pastor, which was a special exception.

When the wedding day finally arrived, we went through security with Mike's family and entered the visitors' room on time. It was important that we get there by 9:00 A.M., because the ceremony needed to be over by 9:30 A.M. The moment Mike and Elise saw each other, they both burst into tears. It really took you out of the environment. I forgot about all the rules and regulations: It felt like a normal wedding. We were in a glass box in the middle of the visitors' room, and from where I stood I could see this one very tough-looking, tattoo-covered inmate who was meeting with his lawyer. I caught a glimpse of him as Mike and my sister were saying their vows, and I saw that he was wiping away tears.

I've been to a ton of weddings, but this was by far the most emotional. With only eight objects and no fancy white dress or poofy veil, its simplicity amplified the joy and happiness of the occasion. I felt blessed and honored to be a part of it.

I'm always anxious, but after the wedding I was in a wonderful mood. Even as I walked out of the prison, knowing that my sister was leaving her husband behind, I had a good feeling about what had happened. But later, when I got home to my husband and my kids, it hit me how much I take for granted, and how hard my sister's situation would be for the next few years. If Elise could be so patient and optimistic, couldn't I be grateful for the blessings in my life?

—A, 45

THE BRIDESMAID'S ASSISTANT

I WAS AT MY OFFICE really late one night planning a friend's bachelorette party—e-mailing realtors about rental houses, tallying up costs, and figuring out dinner reservations—and I thought, "Someone could totally pay me to do this." I bought the domain name maidtothemaids.com right then, and I began developing a small business: I help maids of honor find bridal shower venues, organize bachelorette itineraries, and even plan elements of the actual wedding.

There are a million wedding blogs, but no one is focused on everything the bridesmaid has to do. People forget how much work goes into being a bridesmaid, and I want to be a resource for girls who need help with their obligations. And that doesn't just mean help with planning: Every girl who gets the title of bridesmaid needs fitness tips to get them ready to be in a bathing suit at the bachelorette party, sundress ideas for the bridal shower, ideas of where to go to get their brows done or skin exfoliated before the wedding.

I'm an event planner by day, so being a bridesmaid comes naturally to me. I've been in five weddings, but I think I've devoted years of my life to the planning of all the events. When my best friend got married, I spent about an hour a day on planning during the course of a year. I know everyone doesn't have time for that, which is why I founded the company. Since the bridesmaid is already spending a thousand dollars, minimum, I thought lawyers or doctors—ladies who are short on time but long on income—might be willing to pay to delegate their duties.

If someone hires me, I might research venues and send a brief that the bridesmaid can share with the wedding party, compile prices and make a list of luncheon spots, source favors and centerpieces for a shower, or mediate relations with a pushy mother of the bride. I'm planning a shower in a few months, and I'll be the point person for the vendors and manage the flow of the event, so that the bridesmaids and the bride can just enjoy the day. If a bride doesn't want to play a cheesy game at her shower, but her mother insists that she must, I'll come up with a creative idea like a Chinese auction, so guests win little prizes throughout the event.

I understand that you're supposed to enjoy doing bridesmaid's duties because it's about being a good friend. But that's a little idealistic. So if I'm involved, the bridesmaid can take total credit for my work. At other times the bridesmaids are okay with me being a part of the process. One time I planned a bachelorette night and went along for the whole thing. I got everyone past the doorman, made sure everyone had enough to drink, and collected money at the end of the night. I think people appreciated having a sober person around.

The bachelorette party is perhaps the bridesmaid's biggest obligation. It's a real challenge to plan an awesome bachelorette party while being aware that girls have a million other things to pay for. The last bachelorette party I did was a wine tasting for twenty girls in a house in the North Fork of Long Island. I asked each bridesmaid to pay two hundred dollars, which covered a party bus, the house, some meals, and tastings at three vineyards. The bride wasn't a huge partier, but she still wanted to have a good time, so I planned a tour of the three vineyards ending at a club-like tasting room. There was wine-chugging and dancing on tables at 2 P.M.

I think I'm going to transform the idea of being a bridesmaid. Everything is more elaborate these days, and a bachelorette party is not about a night of binge drinking anymore. When you have to organize ten girls' flights, plus a whole weekend of spa visits and dinners out, you might need a travel-agent-meets-event-planner who'll tolerate the craziness. I'll be that girl, plus a sober guardian on a drunk night out, and a buffer between you and the bride's mother. Bridesmaids might not know they need me, but they do—I hope my little side gig will become a big brand.

—J, 27

THE SCARLETT O'HARA LOOK-ALIKE

PICTURE THIS: The bride is Chinese American, the groom is Italian, and they decide that everyone in their wedding should dress like characters from *Gone With the Wind*. I was a bridesmaid, and we wore ballgowns that didn't quite have hoop skirts, but they had so many ruffled underlayers that the skirts were about six feet in diameter. Once I put on my dress, I could barely navigate a bathroom stall. The dress was sleeveless, with a high ruffled neck and an empire waist. Oh, and there was a sunhat with an oval brim that came over my eyes. Each of us wore a different shade of blue, and our hats matched our dresses.

The whole ensemble might have suited Scarlett O'Hara at a picnic, but it didn't look great on two Asian girls and an Italian bridesmaid who was a hundred pounds overweight. I have no idea how the bride came up with this. We all went to the bridesmaid dress store together, and one of the mothers pulled out the dress and said, "This would look good on everyone." Some other silly soul said, "Yeah, and after you're done you can cut it down to make it into a cocktail dress—you'll wear it again!" I don't think the timeless falsehood "you'll wear it again" has ever been less true. There is no way you could cut down all the frills on this dress. We were all silently mortified, but no one verbalized our mutual horror: This was the worst bridesmaid dress in the world.

It would have been fine if someone had said, "No freaking way." But it's as if we were all speechless. We were outnumbered and we were forced to agree once the bride had made up her mind. I was in my late twenties, in my first turn as a bridesmaid, and I thought that maybe this was part of the deal.

The wedding was outdoors, in a garden. I think this was all to fulfill the bride's storybook idea. She could have had a traditional Chinese wedding, but she wanted to go way Western with the poofy dresses and sunhats. Plus, she was in her early twenties, so this was her idea of a princess moment. I was so horrified with my dress that I barely remember what she wore. I do distinctly remember her train, which was about six feet long. As she walked down the aisle, it picked up every branch and leaf in her path. We called it the leaf catcher. When she went inside she left a forest of twigs wherever she turned.

Her veil was even longer—about twelve feet—and since it was a very windy day it wouldn't stop flying up in the air. We were all watching it as it waved around in the wind, and finally the best man caught it so that I, in my Miu Miu heels, could jump on top of it to pin it down.

Once we had captured the veil, I tried to communicate to the not-so-bright best man that he was standing in front of the video camera that was supposed to be taping the ceremony. I was trying to pantomime all of this without being distracting, and he finally got the message about five minutes before the end of the ceremony.

But the bride was so completely calm. My husband said she could have gotten married in a war zone and it wouldn't have fazed her. And after a few glasses of wine, I was okay too. I was newly married, and I was comforted by the fact that my husband had to love me even if I was wearing the worst dress in the world. If I were there with a date, it would have been a different story.

I kept the dress because it was perfect for my daughter's dress-up games. She would put it on and stomp around like a Southern-style Disney princess. When I finally threw it out a few months ago, I was reminded all over again of its aggressive ugliness.

The funniest thing, in retrospect, was the pictures: They had hired this supposedly professional photographer, but all of the pictures came out with a yellowish tint to them. He had either overexposed the photos or messed up the film, so the only photos the couple has from the wedding day are the ones I took. It was a ridiculous stroke of luck that my wearing that dress was never documented. Because believe me, the blackmail opportunities would have been wild.

—K, 50

THE UNWELL BRIDE

I HAVE A REALLY rare medical condition that we've never been totally able to figure out. Doctors have thought it was a mitochondrial disease, and they've thought it was an autoimmune disease. They're not sure what's going on with me, but I'm really sick. When I was a senior in high school, I had a seizure that lasted four and a half minutes and caused me to lose all of my memory. It happened in a classroom at school, and everyone thought I was dead when the paramedics came and took me away.

When I woke up, my parents had to convince me that they were my parents. They spent months taking me through my photos and yearbooks to reintroduce me to my friends and teachers. I learned that I was so inseparable from my two best friends that everyone called us "the sidekicks." But I hadn't seen them since I was in the hospital. It was like they didn't want to accept the fact that there was something medically wrong with me. I was shipped all over the country for medical treatment, and while I thought these two girls would stick by me through anything, that didn't seem to be the case. My mom called and asked them to come to the hospital once I was near home—instead, they sent me a fruit basket.

That was a disappointment. So when I went to college, I

wanted to make new friends. But my roommate had a bulletin board covered in pictures of her mother giving birth to her, so I decided to pledge a sorority. On bid night—the night when I would potentially accept an offer from the sorority of my choice—I was at the Kappa Alpha Theta house when I got sick. My abdomen was really swollen and I started throwing up in the bathroom. The sorority girls had to call an ambulance, and three upperclassmen were stuck at the hospital with me—they had to call my parents and everything. It turned out I had a ruptured appendix and, being a freshman, I was mortified. But the girls were so nice.

I pledged Theta, and one of those girls ended up being my roommate, Stacy. We became the best of friends—we were workout buddies, and we talked about guys. She hadn't had the best luck with dating, so her mom signed her up for eHarmony. At the time, I was dating a guy who she thought was a douchebag. I'll admit that he was pretty insensitive about my health. She didn't want to be on eHarmony alone, so she asked me to do her a favor: Go out on seven dates in seven days. I told her I didn't have the energy, but she said she'd organize everything—I just needed to show up. All the girls in the house thought it was hysterical.

The guys were a mishmash of people she'd met at college and online. The first night, I met a guy who said he was twenty but was clearly fifty years old. He was trying to smuggle a Russian bride into the country for his brother. I felt like an idiot for having spent such a long time on my outfit and hair and makeup—this guy was a loser. We got in an argument over who would pay the tab, so I just walked out and left him with the bill. The next night was marginally better, but the date was with a Marine who was home for a few days and was just looking for some booty.

By the third night, I was almost done with the experiment.

The guy told me to meet him at a restaurant in the middle of a park, so I drove there and found myself at the end of a one-lane dirt road, in front of a boarded-up restaurant. He pulled up behind me, trapping me in, and I thought, "This is it. I've lived through so many health issues and now I'm going to get murdered in a park?" I called him and said, "Reverse immediately—my doors are locked and you are not getting in this car." Apologetic and panicked, he explained that a friend told him about the restaurant and he had no idea it'd be closed. He asked me to follow his car to a Chinese restaurant on a busy thoroughfare. We sat down, ordered food, and talked until it closed.

The guy asked me on a second date, and of course when the day came I was rushed to the hospital after a seizure. At the time, I was on the waiting list for a whole-organ transplant. That meant that I'd basically be unzipped, and a surgeon would replace everything from the esophagus down, except for the rectum. Every Wednesday I'd go to the transplant clinic and they'd take fifteen tubes of blood. I was just waiting for the phone call that the organs were there, and then I'd be in a really major surgery—I knew exactly what to expect. And even though my new boyfriend didn't know all the details, he had to come to terms with my health early on. Some days, I wake up and I can't even move; other times I'm fine. I take about thirty pills every day, and I have a tube-device in my stomach.

Anyway, this time, I was moved to isolation so that I was only allowed to have family in the room. Another sorority sister, Carly, called the guy to tell him what had happened. He wanted to send flowers, but that's not allowed in isolation because of the potential for bacteria. So he sent the ten ugliest stuffed animals from the gift shop. I was smitten.

Once the girls found out about that, they said, "You're going to marry him." But they were also really protective of me when

I was in the hospital. They were incredibly supportive—my friend Meg even decided to become a trauma nurse after spending so much time with me in the hospital—and with my health being what it was, they thought he needed to prove himself. And from the beginning, he really did.

The day I was supposed to have dinner with his family for the first time, I got kicked off the transplant list. I was getting my weekly blood drawn at the clinic, but all I could think about was the evening ahead. Then my two doctors came in and said I was too weak for the operation. They said I'd die on the table because my heart wasn't strong enough. I didn't have to come to the clinic anymore, and I became terminally ill, which means that sooner or later this illness—whatever it is—will kill me. When I got the news, I was a wreck. I did a conference call with my friends, and they said that nothing had really changed; that there was no point in thinking about it. They encouraged me to go to the dinner with his parents, and I did. A few months later, we were engaged.

You can guess who I chose to be bridesmaids: Stacy, Carly, and Meg. My health has gone up and down during the engagement, but they've been amazing, practically avalanching me with calls and texts—constant check-ins about my health. I have been at a hospital out of state, so the girls have been including my fiancé in all their plans. He's like, "Why did I get asked to see *Twilight* with the girls?"

My bridesmaids realize that while a normal bride could get up early in the morning and do all the getting-ready stuff, I can't be active for all those hours. They came with me to my fittings and practiced getting the dress off of me quickly in case of an emergency: If my stomach tube starts leaking, they can tear the dress off in thirty seconds flat. Meg sent me a picture of the clutches they want to wear with their dresses, and when I told her they looked a little big, she said they needed room for some pills and IV tubes just in case.

I'm not having an IV in my dress even though that's what those mother hens would like. And although I can't remember what I imagined my wedding would be like when I was a little girl, I'm pretty sure I could never have anticipated having such a loving and loyal group of bridesmaids. All I can hope is that I'll be able to repay the favor as a bridesmaid in each of their weddings. And if my overprotective friends have any say in the matter, I think I'll be okay.

—J, 26

THE MUSE

AFTER TEN TURNS AS A BRIDESMAID, I've gotten pretty good at it. Good at telling each bride yes, I will definitely wear this dress again (even though I never, ever will). Good at mastering the rehearsal dinner speeches. Good at making a sweaty fool of myself on the dance floor.

But this isn't a story of the wedding where I wore a white shantung mermaid dress so that I looked like a calla lily, or the toast I made where I inadvertently called the groom a mug (rhymes with his name). This is one about my favorite kind of bridesmaid—the muse.

I had known Mark for ten years. We worked together, and at first I found him really intimidating. One day, we were in a meeting and we discovered that we'd be in Europe at the same time. We decided to travel together even though we'd never even gone out for a drink. It was a risky move, but after a week in Paris, we were best friends. Since then, our only rough patch was when he broke up with his now-husband for a little while. He was nervous about commitment, and I was devastated because I loved them together.

Thankfully, they reunited and eventually got engaged. The wedding was to be held in Palm Springs—aka gay heaven—just months after gay marriage was legalized in California. So it was pretty much the perfect scenario for my first gay wedding.

I was not asked to be a muse—I was invited. You see how much nicer that is already? The grooms sent me an e-mail that said, "In ancient Greek mythology, the Muses were the daughters of Mnemosyne and Zeus. The goddesses inspired all creativity and beauty in literature, science, music, and the arts. The modern definition is 'the goddess or power regarded as inspiring an artist, poet, or thinker; a guiding genius.' For that reason, we have invited each of you to be Muses at our wedding. You are the women who inspire us to be better men." There was a mood board attached to the note that showed ten dresses and a jumpsuit in ivory, gold, and blush, with a legend on the right delineating the appropriate color palette. The muses' dress code was 1970s Halston resort.

I felt like I had been invited to join a secret society. This was so far from being forced to don a dress that had been designed to make the bride look better. No no, I had graduated from all that and was now under pressure to build an entire "look" that would align with an elaborate visual concept. I was faced with the challenge of putting together a newer, better, more fashionable, more sophisticated version of me.

Being the competitive person that I am, and knowing the rush of gay love that would wash over me if I succeeded, I pushed myself to try and be the tallest muse. I obviously had to wear a jumpsuit. I bought many in different shades. I sent pictures of them to the grooms for approval, but I knew the one they would choose: The ivory silk, sheer-back Phillip Lim number with long, wide legs. (The grooms' text reply to a photo of me in the suit: "We knew you could do it!") I also found a blush-colored suede jacket and gold Miu Miu heels.

When all of us muses arrived at the venue—a massive house they had rented—and pulled on our ensembles, the grooms were giddy with excitement. (They wore custom-made suits in light blue and khaki.) The only thing left was my hair. One of the grooms is an amazing hairdresser who had been a major pop star's head stylist. You see what I mean about this being a dream gay wedding? Instead of relaxing on his big day, he opted to create a muse hairstyling factory. There was no question about my hair—we all agreed on tall. So he piled my hair in a top bun. A net donut added oomph.

I have realized that the beauty of gay weddings is that there aren't years and years of precedent, protocol, and history to honor or battle. Today's grooms—and brides—are pioneers, and with that comes freedom. Maybe their mothers don't know whether they can be pushy, or maybe the grooms themselves don't feel they need to go the same-old, tired way of other married friends. Whatever it is, these two put together the most personalized, fun, intimate, and loving wedding I have attended, bar none.

The officiant, their friend, walked down the aisle burning white sage. The song that carried us down the aisle was Nina Simone's "Feeling Good." I don't know what came over me—I'm used to doing the standard step, tap, step at weddings—but I started to slither down the aisle, working in some dance moves along the way. I may have even done a muse meow; it's hard to say.

Later, there was a full-on drag show, featuring one of the grooms and a bunch of his friends decked out in interpretations of bridal dresses. One wore McQueen-style horns, with a veil over them, and the groom looked like Madonna in her "Like a Virgin" days. Some of their friends are big in the drag-queen community, so it was an amazing performance. The finale had everyone jumping into the pool, including both grooms and a few muses. I was wearing ivory silk, so I demurred.

The night ended with one of the groom's fathers—soaking wet in his wifebeater, boxers, and knee-high socks after a dip in the pool—walking around in my pink leather jacket. I was horrified, but not as much as his son and wife were. After peeling it off of him, I retired to my hotel room with muddy, wet silk ankles and my heels and jacket over my shoulder. My wilted look was proof of a great night—I think even Halston would have been proud.

Now when I think of being a bridesmaid, I feel like the role is caged by the word itself—to serve the bride. But being a muse liberates and equalizes it—I loved knowing that I had offered even a tiny bit of inspiration to this amazing relationship. The grooms honored our friendship while expanding the responsibilities of being a bridesmaid from one wedding to a lifetime. On the first anniversary of their marriage, we muses received the following note: "We're in Palm Springs this week, celebrating our anniversary and appreciating all of the beauty, intelligence, and wisdom you bring into our lives. Thank you again for making our wedding the most special day."

—N, 35

THE MAN OF HONOR

I NEVER THOUGHT I'd be consulted for a book about bridesmaids because I'm a straight, twenty-nine-year-old former frat guy. But I have two sisters, which means I've seen *Pretty Woman* seven hundred times, so I wasn't totally fazed when my older sister asked me to be her "man of honor" in her nontraditional wedding. But, man, is it easier to be a groomsman.

From what I've surmised, the groom is responsible for 10 percent of the wedding, and that small portion filters down to the groomsmen. This means all I usually have to do is to wear the right outfit and show up on time; bring a Cuban cigar and a nice bottle of scotch and you've gone above and beyond. But being on the bride's side is a ton of work—90 percent of the work, in fact. It can be very overwhelming.

I knew my sister would need me to be involved in the wedding planning. My dad has his hands full with his second wife, and my mom isn't exactly super hands-on. I could tell that my sister had this fantasy that my dad would want to help her pick out flowers, but that obviously wasn't going to happen, so I wanted to fill the void. We've always been extremely close—perhaps in part because of the divorce—but I still couldn't have predicted what a wedding planner I'd become.

It started with the dress. My sister convinced herself they don't sell wedding dresses in Philadelphia, where she lives, so she came up to New York to try some on. She wanted me there. So I went to sit in these froufrou bridal salons with two other bridesmaids, and I'd weigh in on the dresses. I do think my opinion counted. The girls were very afraid to ask how much all the different dresses cost, and the salesladies in those salons are as distracting and evasive as the shrewdest politician. I'd ask the price and they'd hedge the question and fuss around me, but I'd just ask harder. In the end, it was an easy decision: After she tried on many styles in more than a few stores, all of us knew right away when she found the right dress. My younger sister and I said in unison, "That's the one," and I wondered what had happened to me.

I didn't go to every fitting because after attending two of them, I couldn't handle it. The number of hours she spent inside that store—it was wild. But we still had all this crap to do: I threw her an engagement party, I planned the bachelor and bachelorette parties, I made gift bags in my apartment, I helped plan the logistics of the wedding day.

At times, I felt overwhelmed. It was a destination wedding in Mexico, which made things slightly more complicated. The gift bags were a real pain in the ass. I ordered tote bags, sunglasses, golf balls with the couple's faces on them, sunblock, painkillers, energy drinks, and granola bars. I had to write a note, print it, and fold it into envelopes, which took four hours alone. The bags took a whole weekend to finish, and there was a point when my apartment was filled with tulle and golf balls, with a seating chart stuck to the wall. (I was helping my sister with postdivorce seating diplomacy.) Of course, my friends thought I was totally crazy and posted my girly apartment all over Instagram. They couldn't get enough of my bridesmaid woes.

My sister asked me to pick up the dress and bring it to Mexico. The wary ladies at the bridal store made me wait while they called her to determine whether I could actually be trusted with the dress box. It sat in my apartment for a month leading up to the wedding. At first, I kept it in the closet, but I was afraid it was getting messed up so I started keeping it laid across the floor in my living room (I had read online that it was best to store it flat).

One night, my friend and I had girls over to the apartment without realizing how weird it was that I had a wedding dress in my living room. Things got awkward. The girls just wouldn't believe that it was my sister's, and my friend joked that I was keeping the dress close in case Mrs. Right showed up. They bolted. I made room for the dress in my closet after that.

My sister was definitely grateful for everything I did, but whenever I completed a task and came to her looking for praise, she'd be like, "Oh, great, here are two more things to do." We'd talk by phone a few times a day, and the texting never stopped. She was a text monster. There was a murky line between rhetorical texts and those that demanded answers, and most of her texts were so long that I'd have to call her back. My responsibilities kept getting bigger and bigger over time, but I could see that her stress was mounting. So I just sucked it up and learned how to design a tote bag and about what flowers would be available in Mexico in the fall.

I can see why some bridesmaids get kicked out of wedding parties. So many factors make the planning process stressful, but the hardest thing was that my sister had a picture of what the wedding would be like, and she had to come to terms with everything that didn't quite live up to her expectations. My greatest advantage was that when my sister was being irrational, I could say, "You are completely wrong and you are being completely crazy." She'd hang up on me and then call me back later like nothing had happened. I could be honest with her, which is something only a brother can really do.

When it was finally time to go to the wedding, I had to carry the dress with me on the plane. My sister gave me strict instructions about how to avoid wrinkling it since the hotel couldn't steam it on-site. So I was freaking out. The dress itself wasn't big, but they put so much stuffing in the box that it was huge. I traveled with a friend, and I upgraded him to first class using work miles so that I could ensure two spaces in the overhead bin. He took pictures of me at the Admiral's Club, peeking into the box during our layover.

The rehearsal dinner was on the beach, and we decided to serve skewers of grilled shrimp. All of us were barefoot, and two hours into the dinner my sister got impaled by a skewer that someone had tossed in the sand. She was really hurt, and we were afraid she wouldn't be able to dance at the wedding, but my plastic-surgeon uncle stitched her foot up and gave her antibiotics and a tetanus shot right there at the resort. She said it still hurt the next day but, listen, I think she's also a bit of a wimp.

On the wedding day, it poured for the first time in weeks. We had no contingency plan, so I had to get involved and make things work. We moved the wedding from the beautiful beach spot to a bland hotel reception room. That was a stressful moment, but my sister actually handled it better than I did—I was pretty disappointed after all that planning.

I had to do a toast, and I really tried to write it so that I wouldn't cry. I edited out any potentially sappy parts and rehearsed it several times. I needed to nip any potential for tears in the bud, since the last thing I needed was to be the maid of honor crying in front of all my friends. I did get a tiny bit choked up, but I didn't actually shed any tears, which was a relief.

I'm happy my sister and her husband can look back on their wedding and know that I was able to help them start their new life together. But since the wedding did get rained out, I had this very frustrated, bridesmaidy sense of failing to make everything perfect. And in the end, while some girls might have been like, "Oh, but the flowers and dress looked so pretty," I was thinking about how much money everything cost, and what else we could have done with such a large sum. I'm not even sure if I want a wedding, but if I do, I want to hire a totally crazy wedding planner who would get super stressed and scream at everyone for me. It's the only way I could relax.

—B, 28

THE WEDDING PLANNER

I'M A CLEVELAND-BASED wedding planner, and I've been a bridesmaid twice. For the first bride, my best friend, I put together an itinerary, worked with vendors, planned a bachelorette party, and even helped the groom arrange a wedding-day appearance from Brutus Buckeye, the Ohio State mascot. It was fun for me to help, and I felt like the bride made an effort to treat me like a bridesmaid on the day of the wedding; when things got a little behind schedule she didn't blame me. She even gave me a check at the end, and wrote a lovely note thanking me for all my time and service. I felt appreciated.

My second experience wasn't as positive. When this friend got engaged, she asked me to be a bridesmaid and assumed that I'd plan the wedding, too. So I did, arranging the event from top to bottom. It was challenging because she and her fiancé were so cheap. They wouldn't spring for a bus to take the bridal party from the venue to the reception—even after I got them a discount—so we had to drive ourselves. I had to pick up the flowers on the morning of the wedding to save them a fifty-dollar delivery fee, and when I delivered them to the church and venue, I saw that I'd be expected to do prep work too. When I got to the bridal suite, I had to help the photographer set up his shots. I had about twenty minutes to get into my dress and get my makeup done before walking down the aisle.

Listen, I was happy to help. But one thing really rubbed me the wrong way. I told the couple that they needed to thank the guests for coming. All it would take was the groom standing up for thirty seconds to say he was grateful to everyone for being there. He wouldn't do it, so it fell on the bride. On the wedding day she comes into the venue and says, "My mom said I don't have to thank everyone." I was like, "You're thirty years old! Come on—grow a pair." I just thought it showed a lack of manners, so I thought, "I'm over it," and started drinking gin and tonics (it was a cash bar, of course).

The nicest thing the bride did for me was buy me my bridesmaid dress, but it was twenty dollars on sale at Express. When I put it on, another friend said, "I love you, and you always look great, but that dress makes you look pregnant." At the end of the wedding, after midnight, as I was breaking stuff down and packing it all up, I got my first thank-you. It was from the groom.

I knew they didn't have a ton of money; they were relying on what their parents gave them, and they were trying to save as much of it as they could. But they also invited three hundred people. I see this all the time: "We have X amount of dollars and three hundred people on our guest list; how do we cut costs?" Well, that's pretty easy—just invite fewer people! Little touches and a tiny bit of thoughtfulness would have made the wedding better for the bridal party and the guests.

I've worked with a lot of super-awesome wedding parties who have reminded me what being a bridesmaid is all about. There was a doctor who gave a really heartfelt speech about how much she admired her sister, a stay-at-home mom. There are bridesmaids who constantly check in with me to see what they can do to support the bride. Unfortunately, the jealous perpetual-bridesmaid types are also common. Once I planned a wedding where the bride's sister began her speech by saying, "She's not the good girl you think she is," and I had to shut off the mic. Also: The younger the bride, the more trashed her bridesmaids get at the wedding.

Bridesmaids need to remember that this is a financial commitment: You'll have to spend a couple hundred dollars on shoes, a dress, and a shower. You'll never wear the dress again. If you're in a tight spot, you should really tell the bride before you accept the duty. Money is the biggest bone of contention, but it's also the most easily avoidable.

Brides often forget why they have bridesmaids in the first place. Bridesmaids are not assistants; they're supporters and confidantes. It can be hard to keep brides levelheaded, and I hate seeing some of them go off the deep end. That is part of why I'm getting out of this business. Dealing with people and giving up every Friday and Saturday night can get tiresome, so I'm becoming a teacher. Is it harder to wrangle brides or kindergarteners? I'll let you know.

—K, 28

THE DIVORCÉE

THE TIMING WAS PRETTY HORRIBLE. Three days after my husband told me he wasn't attracted to me, I had to go to my best friend's engagement party. A few weeks later I had to celebrate another friend's engagement—it was the last time my husband and I attended an event together. I couldn't believe my luck: Two of my friends were planning their weddings just as my marriage was falling apart.

My intimacy issues with George had gone back for years. We only had sex regularly during the first year of our three-year marriage. He always had an excuse, and I was always trying to make it work. Neither of us ever cheated or stopped loving each other. And he isn't gay (at least I don't think he is!).

After he told me he wasn't attracted to me, divorce seemed imminent. The last thing I wanted to do was celebrate love. But the one positive thing was that he was out of town for the first engagement party. We had been pretending to be happy for a while, so I was happy to have a break from that. No one knew how bad it had gotten. I put on a hot outfit and went to the party, which was an outdoor affair with candles in mason jars on a beautiful summer night. But the whole time, all I could think was, "My husband isn't attracted to me. Am I going to get a divorce?" I left after an hour and went to see my parents. They had wine ready for me, and I told them everything.

One of the brides-to-be, Maryann, came with me to my divorce lawyer. Three weeks later, I found myself tying bows and cutting stuff and doing all this crap as I helped her invite four hundred people to her wedding. I couldn't believe I was getting divorced. I felt like I had just stuffed my own wedding envelopes and spent hours fussing over invite verbiage. I still remembered that bridal feeling of floating with excitement and brimming with love— when you look around and see all these people who are happy for you, and who wholeheartedly support you and your fiancé. It's such an amazing feeling, and when I saw my friend floating on that cloud, I wanted to die. I excused myself for a minute and went to the bathroom and cried.

The night before Maryann's wedding, I dreamt that I had called off my own wedding. I was really sad when I woke up. I somehow managed all my bridesmaid's duties, and I held it together really well at the wedding—until our song came on at the reception. By this point, I had gotten really good at crying in bathrooms, so I ducked in for a few minutes and emerged feeling slightly better.

I'm not normally gushy, but Maryann and her husband, John, are one of those rare couples who are so wonderful together. I had helped her through some terrible breakups, and I had eaten many frozen pizzas with her on her couch. My first New Year's Eve as a married woman, I spent the night eating fajitas and watching Disney movies with her because her boyfriend had dumped her ass right before Christmas. She had been through hell with men by the time she met John. But with him, it was instantly perfect—they were married within a year. I thought that if I had to go through the silly hoopla of being in a wedding party, I was glad it was for a couple I'd bet the ranch on. After the wedding ceremony, I found myself hoping that I would one day find my John.

I should also say that by this point I hadn't had sex in ages. I had dated a few guys since the divorce, but I hadn't actually done it—and of course George and I didn't have sex for two years before we split. Naturally, I rather drunkenly decided to bring this up to one of Maryann and John's friends at the after-after-party. There were a bunch of us sitting outside on lounge chairs, passing around a bowl of weed, and then it was just me and a friend of the groom's. I divulged my marital woes, and he told me he couldn't get enough sex. He said I was smoking hot and he didn't know what was wrong with my ex. He had a girlfriend, but maybe because of the booze, or maybe because of the weed, our conversation started to sound like it would end in one of our hotel rooms. I was like, "Hmm, is this what I think it is? Is he trying to sleep with me?"

Right after the divorce, during a short-lived bout of optimism, I bought a box of condoms and put some in every purse I owned. If it wasn't for that, I would not have brought him back to my hotel room with me that night. But I was drunk, I was high, I was horny, and I thought, "Why not?" I was like that twenty-year-old who wants to have sex just to lose her virginity. I'm glad I did it without crying or feeling bad about myself, but I do feel weird that I knew he had a girlfriend and did it anyway. I guess I take comfort in the fact that he started it—and the fact that I'll never talk to him again.

At the wedding, watching Maryann and John, I started to realize that my marriage was doomed from the start. George is a great guy in many ways, and he was a wonderful partner to me while it lasted, but, looking back, I knew in my gut that our relationship wasn't right even before we got engaged. I don't know what the line should be between a little problem and a marriage ruiner, but I'm sure that Maryann wouldn't be facing the latter in her union. And that's a huge source of comfort to me.

The wedding came at both the worst and best possible time. Depressing as it was to deal with all the wedding stuff during my divorce, in a way, being a bridesmaid also helped me get through it. I was constantly surrounded by great friends. I was recently talking to my therapist about intimacy and we ended up on the subject of my friends. I surprised myself by getting choked up. I always knew I had good friends, but the support they have shown me this year has blown me away. They've never judged me, even when I was judging myself and worrying about what people would say about me. When I called Maryann to tell her about the hookup, for instance, she didn't care that I had interrupted her honeymoon. She was just glad I had gotten laid.

—D, 33

THE PRINCESS'S BRIDESMAID

I HAD BEEN A BRIDESMAID seven times before Princess Diana's wedding. I don't know why, as I wasn't particularly good at the role. I hated wearing dresses. For me, at age thirteen, Charles and Diana's wedding initially felt like a family affair. Until the day of, when I looked around and saw that I was in a glass carriage driven by horses. That was the moment I woke up.

In England, bridesmaids are chosen because they're close family members, or because they have special relationships with the bride or groom. Prince Charles is my godfather, so he was the one who called to ask me to be a bridesmaid. English bridesmaids are generally children. The role is purely decorative.

In the months leading up to Diana's wedding, there were only hints that it would be the big phenomenon that it was. I was in boarding school in the countryside at the time, without TV or newspapers. I went to London for a couple of rehearsals, and when my car pulled up to the steps of St. Paul's Cathedral, I saw the press lying in wait. I never anticipated that level of interest in me, of all people, a tomboy from the country who just happened to be in Diana's wedding. The father of one of William's page boys recently told me that he debated allowing his son to take part in the wedding because he was worried about him being in the spotlight at such a young age. But seeing all of that excitement through a child's eyes is something special, and you're not thinking about yourself. You're just taking it all in.

That day was just a string of amazing moments. The scale of everything was extraordinary: the number of people outside the cathedral, the uniforms, the drama of the acoustics in the cathedral, Diana's famous dress. The seventeen-year-old Sarah Armstrong-Jones and I were responsible for the twenty-five-foot train, which we had to manipulate into carriages and ultimately down the aisle. At rehearsals, we practiced gently folding a dust cloth tied to Diana's waist. On the day of the wedding, we mostly pushed and creased the train into submission.

The wedding has been incredibly well documented: Diana's three-and-a-half-minute walk down the aisle before 3,500 attendees, her mix-up of Prince Charles' names (she called him Philip Charles instead of Charles Philip). But what I remember most about that day was standing in the cathedral and hearing the vows being broadcast outside. There was a slight delay, and I could hear the crowd scream with excitement when Diana said "and thereto I give thee my troth." Even I was aware of the strange dichotomy: On the inside, we were perfectly behaved, but on the outside, everyone was heaving with joy.

I remember standing on the steps of Buckingham Palace and looking out on the millions of people looking back at me—it was extraordinary. And yet the day was intimate too. We went to what's called a breakfast, which was actually a lunch, and everyone there was basically family since most of the European royal households are interrelated in some way.

At the end, Diana and Charles got into their carriage to ride away as a newlywed couple. Prince Andrew and Prince Edward had tied Coke cans to the back of the carriage, and the queen and queen mother laughed at the cans clanking along behind the royal couple.

At Kate and William's royal wedding, I felt more overwhelmed. I was intimately involved in both in such different ways—for the more recent wedding, I was a correspondent for ABC—and they were similar in that they both fell on spectacular days: The weather fell into place, most unusually for England, and everyone had a good outing and a great celebration. The country came together for both weddings. But at the latter, it was nice to see an older couple who had been together for longer. They managed things internally in a different way, and they were able to give the wedding their own personal touches. That just wasn't possible in Diana's day.

I saw this wedding from a different angle emotionally, but also physically, since I was a part of the media city. Looking back, what I remember most was a moment when I happened to glance up at Buckingham Palace and saw a footman hovering at the edge of the carpet that lined the balcony. This was at the start of the day, before things at the media city began to heat up. The nerves and excitement in his stance—I remember it well.

—INDIA HICKS

THE EX-NUN

MARY AND I BECAME FRIENDS when I was in the novitiate, or novice stage of sisterhood. This was in the 1960s, right after Vatican II, so our religious order was really changing. The order was moving away from the nineteenth century and into the twentieth century, taking on more modern ideas about social justice. Mary and I began working with a farmworkers' union to organize strikes for fair pay. We talked about the changes in the order, and we tried to look at the gospels in terms of the poor.

A few years later, we went to be part of the union's ministry. This was at the height of Cesar Chavez's movement, so it was an exciting time. We felt that we were helping to change the world for farmworkers. We lived in an apartment together and got to know each other really well. But I left the union, and the convent, after a year there. I didn't hate being a nun, but after eight years in religious life, I realized I didn't want to take a vow of chastity.

Mary and I remained great friends when I left, but it was difficult for her to be there by herself. She'd come to visit me, crying about problems with the convent and the union. She is not a very emotional person, but it was a hard time for her. I was twenty-seven, and Mary was thirty-five.

Mary had met a guy, Brad, in high school, and they became

good friends in college. I think they dated a little their first year there, but then they both decided to leave college and join religious life. So he started studying to become a priest, and she entered the convent. They remained friends during their twenty years in religious life—and they really were friends, they weren't lovers. I don't want to give the impression that they were working out their feelings for each other that whole time, because they were both completely dedicated to their orders. But I think this thing between them grew, and she decided to leave the order about four years after I did. He left the priesthood three or four months later, in 1973.

Shortly after, they got engaged. I can't even remember how I heard about the engagement because it was so organic. The same goes for the moment when I knew I'd be a bridesmaid—I think it was just assumed. Mary and I had been close friends for a really long time, and we were also good friends with another former nun, who Mary chose to be the other bridesmaid.

When Brad left the priesthood, he didn't want to do the laicization—or defrocking—because he would have had to say he didn't know what he was doing when he took his vows. It was like an annulment. He loved the priesthood and the community too much to say that, so they couldn't have a church wedding. His brother said he'd throw the wedding in his backyard.

I was going through changes at the time as well. When I left the convent, I was planning on marrying a man and raising a family. But I fell in love with a woman named Lydia. We dealt with a lot, and we were far from "out." I was Catholic, and she was a doctor—and one of only seven women in her class in medical school. We started a clinic in a poor neighborhood, and our patients were mostly Hispanic—and mostly socially conservative. I could have talked to Mary about what I was going through, but I didn't because I was too busy denying it to myself. Recently, she told me that she didn't even know that Lydia and I were in a relationship back then. Which was what I wanted. I was trying to figure things out, but I was also trying to not figure things out.

At that point, I was going to school to become a physician's assistant and working at the clinic I founded with Lydia. I didn't have any money, so I remember being relieved that Mary and Brad bought me the bridesmaid dress. When they went to Mexico to buy the rings, they picked up two of those floor-length Mexican dresses with flowers on them. That's what we wore. We didn't do all the planning and dresses and shoes. We had been in religious life for all these years, and we felt old and mature: I was thirty, and she was not quite forty, but we had already lived another life.

My mom and two sisters drove me to the wedding, which was out of state. An hour before the wedding, I showed up at Brad's brother's house with my sisters and my mom after a day of visiting parks and swimming and running around. I didn't even realize I was making a faux pas. No one really cared, but now I know you're not supposed to attend a wedding unless you're specifically asked!

Mary borrowed her friend's wedding dress, and they were married by an ex-priest. They are spiritual, thoughtful people, so the ceremony incorporated God, and their commitment to God and justice. There was a disconnect because all of these people at the wedding were good Catholics, and there were a few ex-nuns and ex-priests there, but the wedding couldn't be blessed by the Catholic Church. These days, people are more comfortable with breaking tradition at weddings. But then, they stepped out of tradition only because they needed to.

Still, they seemed really happy. Mary was so elated, so in love, and she had such anticipation about the life she and Brad would have together. And now, forty years later, we're still the closest of friends. They have stayed in the church, and they raised their daughter in the church. Lydia is her godmother. We live down the street from each other, and our lives are completely entwined.

Just a few weeks ago, Lydia and I got married after the Defense of Marriage Act was struck down. Mary, Brad, and their daughter were three of the fifteen people at the ceremony. There was a parallel between our marriage and theirs, in that we both dealt with a measure of unacceptance. They weren't embraced by the church, and for years Lydia and I felt that we weren't fully embraced by society. I'm not one for breaking the rules, but you love who you love. When you're faced with rejection, you have to decide whether you'll follow the rules. We all decided to go our own way.

—B, 70

THE SMALL-TOWN SOUTHERNER

WHEN SARAH AND I WERE SEVENTEEN, we went to a house party and she disappeared into a bedroom with this guy. She lost her virginity, and nine months later, she had a baby girl. It was one of those classic stories. In our tiny town in Alabama, it was also a life sentence: Everyone assumed she'd get married, stop school, and spend the rest of her life in the South. But that wasn't what she did. Her parents took care of the baby, and she went to college. She was motivated and had initiative. I was so proud of her.

Her freshman year of college, Sarah fell in love with Jeff. He was a sweet, genuine guy from a good family. I can say this first-hand because I dated him in high school. His family was Mormon or something—they didn't drink or really have any kind of fun at all—and he was seen as this knight in shining armor. Everyone said she got so lucky to find a man who would marry her and take care of her. He got a job that at the time seemed to pay a ton of money—when you're twenty, thirty grand a year feels great. So they both dropped out of school.

Shortly after, Jeff lost his job. And then he started drinking. By the time the wedding rolled around, he had several DUIs on his record and Sarah, who was prone to anxiety, was through the roof. As a bridesmaid, I became her emotional caretaker. We had been friends since we were four, and we had both struggled with anxiety and depression. She cried from the minute she got engaged to the minute she got married, and I was very involved in helping her manage it—she was mostly nervous that it would all come apart. She thought she was lucky to have found a man to take care of her, and she worried that if he found out about all of her problems, he would back out.

I never even considered that maybe *she* should have been the one to back out. I thought the alcohol stuff was a lapse—after all, I had dated him, and I believed he was a nice, nice guy—and I'm ashamed to say I bought into the idea that Sarah was lucky to find someone to take her on. I was too young to think with more complexity. Plus, the wedding was so exciting. It was our first one, and we were all thrilled about being bridesmaids. There were seven of us, and it was like a popularity contest: Being a bridesmaid was like wearing a badge that said "People like me!" We got fitted in strapless, deep-green gowns that looked like prom dresses. I thought they were beautiful.

On the day of the wedding, we went to a salon to get our hair done. We were supposed to get updos, but I asked for a cut and color—and a manicure and a pedicure too. The wedding was in two hours, so there clearly was not time for this, and Sarah hated me for it. But my feelings were hurt and my ego was bruised; I both wanted to be the bride and felt jealous that she had become closer to the other bridesmaids. It was so selfish of me. I just did what I wanted, and I got a terrible color and cut. I had such a propensity for doing that at the time that my therapist said my crazy haircuts were a form of self-mutilization: Whenever I felt sad or out of control, instead of cutting myself, I cut my hair.

I was an hour late leaving the salon, and Sarah wasn't speaking to me. But by the time I got to the plantation where the wedding was to be held, she had popped a few "nerve pills," or Xanax, and she was high as a kite. At every Southern wedding I've been in, someone has been jacked up on Xanax—if not the bride then at least her mother.

It was a dry reception, which wasn't unusual in the South. But in this crowd, where so many had dedicated their lives to drinking, having a dry wedding was way too much. Jeff's relatives might have been teetotalers, but Sarah came from a family of alcoholics—which explains why she married one. Anyway, her mother brought bagfuls of vodka and other things into the bridal parlor, and every five minutes or so we'd go upstairs and chug from the bottle, and then come back down. I'm sure Jeff's grandparents were wondering why we were acting so silly. It was because we were secretly hammered.

It was necessary, though, because there wasn't a band or even a DJ. There was karaoke. Sober karaoke was definitely the most depressing part of the whole thing, but once we'd drained a bottle of vodka, we were all on the dance floor. I remember all of us bridesmaids singing "Come On Eileen." By the middle of the party, the only people who weren't drinking were some of the groom's family and their church members—everyone else needed to take the edge off.

A lot of people were coupled up, and I wasn't seeing anyone at the time. I had heard all about the bridesmaid experience where you pick up one of the groomsmen, and I intended on staying very much in line with tradition. I caught the bouquet, and Jeff's brother caught the garter belt, and therefore we made out on the dance floor. The next morning, we were all hungover when we bid the wedded couple adieu. Jeff had so many DUIs that they couldn't leave the state, so they had their honeymoon in Tuscaloosa.

I was the next one to get married, when I was twenty-three.

Sarah's experience didn't make me pause, but it should have. My mind didn't work that way yet, though, and I married an amazing man—he was so super smart and wonderful that I felt like I'd hit the jackpot. I had no qualms, no second thoughts, no anxiety. It never even occurred to me that small issues could become large enough to ruin our marriage; I only figured that out years later, when we got divorced. Sarah, on the other hand, is still married. Jeff is a manager at a Goodyear store and she drives him to work because he lost his license. I have to say that I wish she had somehow escaped the South.

—J, 45

THE OLD 'MAID

IN THE BEGINNING, it was the 1980s. Everything was big, and the color of the moment was mauve. The biggest lesson of the decade was this: Friends should not let friends wear mauve. But in a lot of ways, things were simpler in those pre-reality-TV days. Back then, being a bride wasn't an excuse to act like a raging bitch. A bride would have a shower and a hen night, not twelve showers and a weekend in Vegas. And a wedding was a dinner and dancing, not three days of rehearsal dinners, lunches, after-parties, and breakfasts.

Do I sound like an old grump? I'm really not, but a few years ago I did have the somewhat indecorous experience of being a bridesmaid at the ripe age of . . . well, in my late forties . . . and it made me think about how things have changed since my first weddings back then. I have been a bridesmaid twenty times in thirty years, so I'm no novice, but as the years have worn on I have seen weddings balloon into a crazy expensive business. Most recently, I also realized that there's so much more that you need to do as you get older in order to get ready to stand up in front of your family and friends in a dubious-looking dress. Shoulder pads and lipgloss aren't enough at my age.

The bridesmaid trials I've been through have made me

hypervigilant about how I appear when I march down the aisle. There was the family wedding where I let the makeup artist and hair stylist do their thing, and as I was making my way to the front of the church—with the tunes of Vivaldi wafting in the background—I could hear an elderly aunt loudly whisper, "Oh my god, is that her?" When I was a little older, I was a pregnant bridesmaid, but we didn't do that cute baby-bump thing in my day. I was fat, and I could see people staring aghast at my largeness as I approached the chuppah (this was a Jewish wedding). At the time, all I cared about was making it through the ceremony without throwing up.

I've come to think of being a bridesmaid as making a walk of fame—or a walk of shame—down the aisle. You see family members every few years at weddings, and you want them to think "She lost weight," not "She let herself go." When I'm a guest at a wedding, there's an endless commentary in my head about what people look like. I can't be the only catty one, so when I walk to the front of a church I picture it as my runway moment—I imagine people mentally assessing me using numbers from one to ten. When you're walking down the aisle, it's strictly yours. Depending on its length, you could have a good few minutes in the limelight.

So before my last wedding, I began preparing months in advance. My dermatologist and I made a plan to do the ideal sequence of laser treatments, Botox, fillers, and Juvéderm. I began exercising with a trainer to make sure I'd look good in the dress. I considered my underwear options and chose the pair of Spanx that would serve me best. It took a whole production to make me look presentable—but when I was actually up at the altar, I realized how wide-eyed I'd been as a young bridesmaid. This time, I heard the vows as "I'm going to love you even when you leave wet towels on the bathroom floor, even when your mother annoys me, and even when you can't remember to put the toilet seat down"—which is certainly not what I thought at my own wedding at age twenty-two. (I'm still married, by the way.)

In addition to the mauve lesson, and the dermatologist lesson, I have gleaned some other gems in my tenure as a bridesmaid. One piece of good news is that you're more likely to rewear your dress when you're an older bridesmaid, since older brides are more charitable with their color and style choices. When ordering male strippers, one should always stipulate her target height and weight or prepare to be disappointed by an unappetizing oaf. And as you near the wedding date, watch the bride for pharmaceutical abuse: The only wedding I've been in that ended in divorce was one where the bride popped a Valium or two before walking down the aisle. If the bride needs something stronger than a cocktail, maybe she should hold off on getting married.

In this age of bridezillas and TLC, I'm glad that my bridesmaid career has finally drawn to a close. But my wedding concerns surely aren't over. I'm a mother to two teenaged boys, and I'm already preparing my mother-of-the-groom strut.

—M, 51

THE MORMON

WEDDINGS ARE HUGE FOR MORMONS, literally and figuratively. I had six hundred people at my wedding, and each of my seven older sisters had about that many at her wedding too. But other than being physically large, weddings are a big deal because you can't go to most of the rooms in the temple before you are married, and you can't attend a wedding until you've had one of your own. When you get married, you are blessed and anointed in a very secret ceremony. You also receive what we call garments, which are a symbol of modesty. Garments are a tank top and bike-short-like bottoms that Mormon men and women have to wear under all their clothes.

Mormons get married really quick. It's because of the no-sex-till-marriage thing. If you find someone you really like and you date for a year, people are like, "Okay, so what's the deal? Why aren't you married yet?" After three or four months, you either get engaged or you break up. Almost everyone I know has gotten married after dating for less than nine months. This extraconsolidated time line obviously changes the dynamic of relationships: People get married because they can't wait any longer to have sex, but sometimes they don't know their partners very well.

I have a strong testimony with my church, but I do have an

issue with this aspect of Mormonism. You see these nineteen-year-olds getting engaged after three months of dating, which really bugs me. Divorce rates have been kinda high among Mormons as a result. My eldest sister had a quick marriage and an equally quick divorce, so the rest of us learned from her mistakes. But it was still hard when I dated my now-husband, because he was divorced. It was difficult for him to return to celibacy after marriage—he had to reprogram himself. In order to remarry, he had to go through a year of repentance. So we dated for a year and a half. We knew we wanted a temple ceremony, so we were able to be disciplined, but it was a really huge and hard thing. We both understood that sex is a big part of a relationship.

There's a seventeen-year age difference between me and my oldest sister, so the first time I was a bridesmaid I was seven years old. All of the weddings are blurs of dancing and excitement, and some of the dresses we wore back then were terrible. Two brides had us wear these big sparkly prom skirts, another put us in all black with scarves, one had us in different shades of blue. The worst was when we wore these yellow corduroy things with pearl buttons from the Gap. I don't know what we were thinking!

Garments make the bridesmaid dress a bit of an issue: You need a dress with thick straps to cover the tank top. When half of your bridesmaids are already married, there's a question of whether they'll take their garments off to wear the dress, or whether the bride will choose to have two different dresses—one for those who are married, and another for single girls. People will gossip about girls taking their garments off for someone's bridesmaid dress.

Between my sisters, my husband's sisters, and my friends, I had sixteen bridesmaids at my wedding. Most of them had garments. So the married bridesmaids wore a skirt, blouse, and sweater from J. Crew, and the unmarried girls wore sleeveless navy dresses. Skirts are a popular option for Mormon bridesmaids because it's easy to find blouses that cover the garment.

Since I had been a bridesmaid so many times before my own wedding, I was dying to know what went on in the temple. It's hard inviting non-Mormon friends to weddings because they can't know what's happening, and they have to wait outside during the ceremony. But in a weird way it also makes marriage feel more special. And temples usually have beautiful grounds so guests can always wander around until the ceremony is over. It doesn't take longer than forty-five minutes. After that, you go to lunch with your family and close friends, and later at night you have the big reception.

There's this Utah stereotype of having punch and cookies at the church house after the wedding—that the reception is the opposite of weddingish and is basically a church party. Thankfully none of my friends have had that kind of wedding, but sometimes people have to in order to make the logistics easier. There's pressure to invite everyone in your ward, or church community, which is how the numbers can balloon out of control. And then you'll invite one person to a wedding and he'll bring his wife and six kids. I had dreamed of having an intimate dinner for my reception, but my mother insisted on inviting all these random people. You can't imagine how weird it is to have to introduce yourself to hundreds of people at your own wedding, but since I was the last to get married in my family I didn't have much of a choice.

Of course, the receptions are dry, which saves on costs. But since you still have to feed hundreds of people, almost all Mormon weddings are buffets. My wedding was really expensive—we had great food and cake for six hundred people, after all—but that was my parents' choice: They wanted it to be a social event. My favorite part of the weekend was the rehearsal dinner, which was only for people I actually knew.

—K, 30

THE ALMOST BRIDESMAID

I ALWAYS KNEW I'd be Suzanna's maid of honor. We had been best friends for eleven years, and neither of us had sisters. We were practically inseparable for most of high school. So when she got engaged to her college sweetheart, I was excited to help with the wedding despite the fact that I had been in a really serious ski accident about six months before. I was still struggling with physical setbacks, so I thought it would be a great distraction for me.

She was living in San Diego and I was living in Marin County. She asked three other girls to be in the wedding—it was going to be so much fun! Two weeks after the engagement, Suzanna e-mailed me with a list of forty-five things she expected me to do as her maid of honor. Items included: getting her wedding dress dry-cleaned after the ceremony and making sure it was returned to her house before she was back from her honeymoon, flying to San Diego for every dress fitting and every meeting at the venue, previewing my speech with her before I gave it at the wedding, and of course planning the shower and the bachelorette party. I wrote back, "Haha, this is so funny! This really made my day." But the list was no joke. That e-mail was the beginning of all the bad blood that would come between us.

Suzanna called. She was serious. Could I handle this job? I told her I was still so excited to be a part of her wedding, but that I couldn't be as present in Southern California as she wanted. I had just started my first job as a nurse, and it was really hard for me to get time off. She said she understood. But when I called to tell her I had booked a weekend to come help her try on dresses, she said it wasn't enough—she needed me to be there for a week. That just wasn't feasible given my work schedule, and she started screaming at me. She said that nursing doesn't matter and that my job wasn't important. It upset me so much.

After that, I couldn't have a conversation with her without getting into an argument. She was constantly asking me why I wasn't visiting her and helping her with all the planning—she even called and texted my boyfriend to tell him what a horrible friend I was for not doing anything to help. One day she called to yell at me for not coming to visit her, and she was clearly trying to incite a reaction out of me. When I wouldn't take the bait, she got so upset. She told me that her fiancé was listening in on the line, and that he thought I was crazy too. I really liked him up to that point, but I felt so embarrassed, and angry, that he would listen in on the call.

The whole time I was dealing with her, I was still recovering from injuries related to the skiing accident. I was also on steroids, which made me gain weight. One day, we went to brunch with a bunch of friends. I ate my meal really fast and someone joked, "Do you want my plate too?" Everyone laughed, but Suzanna was like, "Yeah, you're getting really fat and you better lose weight before my wedding." The table went totally silent. Another friend who's a nurse explained that steroids make you really hungry, which sort of eased the tension, but it was still mortifying. (For the record, I'm five foot ten and I weighed like 150 pounds at the time, so it wasn't like I was obscenely fat.)

I knew it wasn't my friend Suzanna talking; I knew that something strange had come over her. I should have put my foot down, but then she fell back into being her normal self, so I cut her some slack and just kept on taking her abuse. I didn't want to ruin the wedding.

My mom and I were planning the shower, so we had been in touch with her and her mom about the invitation list, the venue, the flowers, and the favors. Once we had all the RSVPs and the decorations ordered, I got an e-mail from Suzanna. She had re-placed me as her maid of honor; if I still wanted to be a brides-maid I could be, but that was up to me. She said I couldn't give her the attention she deserved, and that I couldn't help her with everything she needed for the wedding.

I was really hurt, and I was especially upset that she did something like this through e-mail. After speaking to my par-ents and some friends, I decided not to be a bridesmaid. She was really angry about that. It completely ruined our friendship. We saw each other soon after at a mutual friend's bachelorette party, and she wouldn't even speak to me. My mom and I paid for most of the shower even though we were no longer invited. Neither of us got a thank-you note—or even a call—from her mother. My parents were disinvited to the wedding.

My boyfriend and I were still invited to the wedding, but we decided not to go. It was a really hard decision, but he didn't understand how I could even think about going—he was more upset about the whole thing than I was. My reasoning was that Suzanna and I had a great friendship for a long time, and I didn't want to throw that away. But at the end of the day, I didn't want her to be uncomfortable or upset when she saw me there, so I decided it was best for us not to go.

A few months after the wedding, Suzanna called my boy-friend to tell him that she had been diagnosed with Borderline

Personality Disorder. I knew that planning the wedding brought out this whole new person in her that wasn't there before, but I didn't realize how serious it was. It was really sad for me to find out like that. She asked him to tell me about the diagnosis, and to say she was sorry. He said that it was her job to apologize. She never called. The only time I've ever heard from her was a year after the wedding, when she sent me a card thanking me for the china I had sent off her registry: "Thank you for your gift of plates for my home. They look great."

I'm engaged now, and I had hoped that planning my own wedding might make me better able to understand what happened to Suzanna. It hasn't at all. I'm Type A, so I could definitely turn into a mess before it's all said and done, but my fiancé and I have worked together to slowly and steadily plan things, and to keep each other grounded while we do. And every time I see my bridesmaids, I give each of them a little gift and a big hug.

—H, 27

THE TEXAN'S ACCESSORY

THE FIRST TIME I met Martha, I was in a conference room on my first day of orientation. I was starting a cardiology fellowship, and everyone was exchanging pleasantries when in walks this woman with big red hair. She puts her hand on her hip and says, "I'm Martha Maybury. I'm from Irving, Texas. I heard the best of the best are going to be here." I thought, "Thank God there's someone funny here." It was a line from *Top Gun*.

Martha is from the oil fields, but she's not from oil money. Her dad is a lawyer, and her mom is a musician. Martha is gregarious and outspoken—the life of the party. And very Texan. She never leaves the house without makeup; she only wears tennis shoes when she's going to the gym. I was raised by Mexican immigrant parents on a mountain in Oregon. I'm a low-key tomboy, but we still got along great.

After we had been friends for about a year, Martha went away for a monthlong rotation. Two weeks in, she called me sounding really depressed. She hadn't met anyone there; she wondered why she'd ever left. I asked her what she was doing. She was at a bar drinking a glass of Chardonnay and reading an article about SARS in *The New England Journal of Medicine*. I told her to put the journal in her purse and look to her right—was there anyone there? No. Okay, then to her left? There was a guy sitting next to her. I said, "Drink half your wine and talk to that person. Don't call me again until you've made friends." And then I hung up on her.

Three years later, they were engaged. After he proposed, she took me out to dinner, and when I got there, she was waiting with a glass of champagne. She said, "Without you I wouldn't have met Brian; will you be my maid of honor?" I was flabbergasted and surprised because Martha has many friends. But of course I said yes.

Martha was thirty-six when she got engaged, which is quite unusual for a Texan. Her dad had always told her that she wasn't married because she was too fat. She's not fat in any way, shape, or form—she somehow balances a gig as a fitness instructor with her clinical-care and research work. But she was the only girl in the family, so the wedding was highly anticipated. That's probably why there was so much pressure.

By this point, she was living with her fiancé in San Francisco, and she found a wonderful venue there. Her parents were okay with this up until the day before she booked the church. They were Skyping about the wedding and all of a sudden her dad got this look on his face. Being a lawyer, he has a practiced poker face, and within seconds he went from calm and cool and collected to so pissed off: "This is unacceptable! We are having the wedding in Irving. How could you even think about having it somewhere else? Can't you understand that this wedding is not about you?" From then on, this wasn't a case of the crazy mother of the bride; it was all about the dad.

Any bachelorette party I had attended was about going for drinks, or maybe having a nice dinner. But Martha wanted a big, destination bachelorette party, and when she told me as much I wasn't surprised in the slightest: I get her. She wanted me to invite twenty-five women, but we were scattered all across the country, so I settled on New York because it was meaningful to her. She lived there for three years and made friends with a group of female residents who called themselves "the sharks."

You'd think that a bunch of women in their late thirties wouldn't go as over the top as women at a twentysomething's bachelorette party would. But actually, because we could afford more, we went all out: We ate an amazing meal at Indochine— one of New York's coolest restaurants—we took a belly-dancing class, we stayed in a chichi brand-new hotel, we went bar crawling on a party bus. But drinking heavily and staying up past midnight wasn't as easy as it once was: Martha gave us all Tums (for drinking-associated heartburn) and 5-hour Energies, which she insisted we slam at the end of dinner. We made it to 2:00 A.M., and one of the girls was so wired that she didn't sleep a wink! I think we might have been slightly more ridiculous than a group of younger girls would have been: You get twenty strong, independent, opinionated, successful women together and things are going to get a little crazy.

Martha's parents pulled some major strings, and the wedding was the first event to be held in Irving's new convention center. It was like a Who's Who of the city. Martha's guest list started at 350 people—but so did her dad's. Eventually, they were able to whittle both of them down. The wine was flown in from France; the cookies were from New York City; the late-night donuts were from Portland. The Irving Symphony Orchestra accompanied us down the aisle, and then there were these huge drums that sounded like thunder. While they were playing, the doors swung open, and Martha walked in. God, was it dramatic.

My footwear of choice is Danskos—I have ten pairs—but I bought a pair of Jimmy Choos for the wedding. Martha loved that, but I was terrified of falling. My dress was a mermaid cut, so I had this elaborate vision of me falling and splitting the back of it, revealing the Spanx underneath. That didn't happen, but when I was straightening Martha's veil and train, I accidentally dropped her veil on a votive candle for a second. I had a panic attack and immediately envisioned a huge fire. That didn't happen either, and I was so relieved that I burst into uncontrollable laughter once I took my place at the altar. I couldn't stop, so I grabbed a bunch of Kleenex and pretended to cry hysterically.

All the Texan ladies wore feathery fascinators in their hair, and Martha went around with a magnum of champagne, topping off everyone's glass even though there was a whole catering staff. Every guest got a pair of sunglasses emblazoned with a Texas star, the words SUNGLASSES AT NIGHT, and the wedding date; at one point, everyone on the dance floor had them on, and we had the longest conga line I've ever seen. Oh, and there were ten minutes of fireworks at the end of the night. Everything was big and dramatic; very Texan, very her. I spoke to her dad after the fireworks, and I've never seen such giddiness in such a stern and scary man. He was very proud of her, but the moment was bittersweet: He was more proud of this massive wedding than he was of her accomplishments.

I'm divorced, and my wedding cost $18,000, all in all. Martha's wedding cost at least $100,000—the bachelorette party alone cost $10,000. It's easy for people to judge such an extravagant affair, but I think it was worth it. Yeah, you can think of all the things you can buy with that money, but I didn't even know an event could mean so much to someone until I took part in this wedding. It was as much about her parents as it was about Martha—the wedding reflected the family and the state along with her personality. I think it was the right thing.

—O, 38

THE SELF-PROCLAIMED
PROFESSIONAL

MY MOM WAS THE FIRST ONE to call me a professional brides-maid. I had been in four weddings, and at the fifth, my parents noticed that I was the only bridesmaid who knew to stop at the end of the aisle so my groomsman and I could have our picture taken. I sort of casually pulled him to a stop and gave the camera a good smile. My dad said to my mom, "She's the only one smiling!" and my mom said, "Of course she is—she's a professional."

My thing is that I take a positive spin on everything. I wanted a blog, and I had been in so many weddings that the idea just came to me—to blog about being a professional bridesmaid. My site is confessionsofaprofessionalbridesmaid.com. I'm twenty-six and I've been in seven weddings so far, but I'll be in three more in the next six months. For every wedding, I've gone to at least one shower, a bachelorette party—all have been a weekend away—a rehearsal dinner, and then the day itself. I buy plane tickets and hotel rooms for all the events, dresses (they're usu-ally around $350), and gifts for the engagement, shower, and wedding. I'd say I pay around $2,000 per wedding, maybe more.

It takes a good bride to have good bridesmaids. The bride needs to care about her friends, needs to be aware of her brides-maids' budgets and time. And then there are the bridesmaids. If you're complaining, remember that it's not your wedding. It's like, you're supposed to be her best friend, you shouldn't be saying those things. Too often, bridesmaids get caught up in the drama, and you have to remember that the friendship remains after the wedding. I know people who have lost friends as a result of being a bridesmaid. It's the bride's day, and she only gets one of these.

A big part of being a bridesmaid is planning a bachelorette party. I love parties and brunches and getting dressed up, so I love bachelorettes. This is your time to show the bride how much you care about your friendship. For the last one I went to—it was in Austin—we developed more than a thousand pictures and pasted them all over the bride's hotel room. It was the best moment ever when she saw what we had done—she was crying and overjoyed. It's that sort of thing that has strengthened my friendships with my married friends on an entirely different level; I'll always be able to look back and say, "I was a part of that."

When my boyfriend proposed last March, I immediately thought about who my bridesmaids would be. I have a lot of great friends, but I somehow narrowed my list down so I'll have twenty bridesmaids. I wouldn't want to leave anyone out. But I know how much work you put in when you're a bridesmaid, so I want to make sure they feel appreciated. To ask my friends to be in the wedding, I threw a Tiffany-themed brunch. I bought Tiffany-blue bags, invitations, boxes, and even M&Ms, and everything was printed with TRACI & CO. It was a magical day.

I hope my friends realize that I wouldn't be where I am today—engaged—if it wasn't for them. To make them feel even more involved, I invited all the bridesmaids to help pick out the dress. And lucky for me, everyone seems to love it.

—T, 26

THE KISSING BANDIT

"UGH, HERE WE GO AGAIN." I'm sad to say this was essentially my reaction when my best friend from college told me she was engaged. I was excited for her, but I had been in six weddings in the years leading up to this; it was a big period of everyone walking down the plank. I had bridesmaid burnout, and I had it bad. Even though I hadn't had any bridezilla experiences, I kept expecting one—every time I was in another wedding I thought, "Will this be the friend who goes nuts?"

I was also having a quarter-life crisis. I had dated a guy for five years, from the time I was nineteen until I was twenty-four, and when we were twenty-two he caught a flesh-eating bacteria in his leg. He had to have his leg amputated from the knee down—it was a really harrowing experience. When he got a clean bill of health, I was so thankful. I saw this as a time to embrace life. But he had this incredible bitterness: He wanted to drink and smoke his feelings dead. I needed more than that, and slowly I fell out of love with him. Eventually, I packed my clothes and the cat and moved to New York City.

In that, my twenty-fourth year, I was known as the kissing bandit. My main objectives were reclaiming my twenties and blowing off steam. New York had this magical mystique, and when I got there I was just so happy. It was one of the most fun periods of my life. I knew I needed to get more serious, but before I could really start to think about the future, my friend convinced me to go back to the camp where we had worked during summers in college. So we returned as supervisors, and I began cavorting with a cabin counselor. He was twenty, and I was technically his boss. When he told me he was in love with me, I got swept up and blurted, "I love you too!" And then, in a real lapse of judgment—after we had a melodramatic end-of-summer good-bye in the rain (seriously!)—I booked a plane ticket to visit him. It was only when I woke up in his college dorm room that I realized we weren't going anywhere. I went back to New York to try to pump myself up for the wedding, which would be held a month later on Block Island. But first, I promised myself I wouldn't date anyone for at least a year.

Luckily, the bride was lovely and had no expectations for us bridesmaids. It was drama-free. Minus the drama I created for myself, of course. At the rehearsal dinner, I reconnected with an old guy friend whom I had traveled with years before. We had always been totally platonic, but that weekend we kicked it up a notch. I went home with him after the rehearsal dinner.

When I saw him at the wedding the next day, I was wearing my hideous bridesmaid dress. It was this awful satiny seafoam fabric, with a tight mermaid shape and a sweetheart neckline. Only about 1 percent of women could pull that thing off. The bridesmaid who looked best in it was pregnant, which is saying something. Anyway, I fulfilled my bridesmaid's duties by doing a couple of shots of tequila at the reception, and I found my night-before hookup flirting with another girl. In my drunken state, this was inexcusable and unacceptable to me. I marched up to him in a cavalier way and unleashed a stream of ridiculousness—slurring about how he didn't deserve me and how he wasn't treating me with the proper respect. He was understandably baffled, and I became predictably emotional.

I found a friend and started bitching and moaning, and maybe even crying a little on his shoulder. I don't perfectly remember exactly what happened next, but this friend maintains that he said something like, "I have someone you're going to meet. You guys are going to date and it's going to be something for real." I said, "You're wrong. But I'll meet him." I sat down next to Greg at the bar, and I had the easiest conversation I'd ever had with a guy. We chatted for hours, and I went home with him to the cottage he had rented with a bunch of friends. We just kissed, I promise! And then we passed out.

The next day he asked whether he could get a ride with me back to New York. I was like, "Who is this scrub who didn't think ahead?" But given that I was incredibly hungover, I said he could come if he did most of the driving. My friends thought it was a good idea—one five-hour car drive was like three dates in a row. But first I had to get back to the wedding hotel to retrieve my suitcase. I could not walk-of-shame in my seafoam satin dress. So he gave me some of his clothes to wear and I walked into the fanciest hotel on the island wearing men's corduroy pants and a Yankees jersey, hugging my ugly-ass bridesmaid dress to my chest. It was really classy.

On the drive home, conversation was effortless. We talked about families, our pasts, I don't know what else. When we got to the city five hours later we realized we hadn't turned on the radio, which is huge because we are both into music. After that, we started hanging out and things built over time. I never really mourned my self-prescribed single period because I didn't want to be single—I wanted to be with him. And after a few weeks of dating, I found out that he had skipped out on a plane ticket to drive back with me. He thought he might like me and he wanted to spend time together.

Four years later, we got married. I let my bridesmaids wear whatever they wanted. I invited the friend who had sat me down next to Greg, of course, and we had a Quaker ceremony, so the congregation was invited to speak. He stood up first and said, "I'd like to think that I was a tool in you two getting together. I mean that I'm responsible for this whole thing—not that I'm a tool."

—L, 32

THE IRANIAN AMERICAN

IT'S NOT TRADITIONAL to have bridesmaids in Persian weddings, so my brother's fiancée wasn't going to have them at first. But then her pushy sister was like, "No, you have to have bridesmaids! I'll be so hurt if you don't." So the bride asked me to be a part of the wedding. Sure, I said—especially when I heard that we didn't have to wear bridesmaid dresses.

Well, two months before the wedding, the sister insisted that we had to wear matching dresses. And that the color had to be silver. So we began this frantic hunt for silver bridesmaid dresses. We ordered a few that weren't right, and tried on dozens that the bride didn't like. Eventually, she found a dress that struck her fancy—and it was $800. We got a discount, so it came to $480. It was a beautiful strapless silver dress that I could definitely wear again, but that's the most I've ever paid for a dress. Ever.

My siblings and I were born in Iran, but we grew up in America. We're all Americanized Iranians. Same with the bride's family. It's important to my family that we kids marry other Iranians, so they were happy about the union between my brother and his fiancée. It wasn't an arranged marriage; we're not religious like that. They met in high school, and after some on-again-off-again business, they got engaged.

It was the sister who was really the problem. Her ideas about the wedding seemed to be based on what she had seen in the movies. For the bachelorette party, she and the bride wanted to go to Hawaii. That was ridiculously expensive, and I talked them out of it. So the sister says, "Let's just get a suite in Miami for a weekend." Oh, okay, that's really affordable, thanks.

The number of attendees dwindled, they changed the weekends twice, so a month and a half before we were set to go we didn't have anything planned. Every time I offered to plan something, the sister would freak. Finally she hired a party planner to plan this weird party-girl Miami weekend that none of us needed: She planned a night at a strip club, and we had reserved tables at an all-day pool party and an all-night club. When I heard about that twenty-four-hour-party plan, I suggested that we'd be dead tired after drinking all day by the pool—and drinking at the strip club the night before—so there was no need for a table at night. The sister disagreed, and I was right: No one wanted to go drink at the club on Saturday night, so we basically wasted two bottles of vodka—or $1,200.

The suite was $500 per person for the weekend, and plane tickets were $400. So I spent $900 before I set foot in one of the most expensive cities in America (for bachelorette parties, at least). In all, I spent $2,500 on the long weekend, making it the most expensive four days of my life. I was so annoyed with the sister. The bride wasn't involved, and I didn't want to drag her into it. Every time I questioned costs, the sister would brush me off and mention other things in my life that I was spending money on. I hate that.

When the wedding rolled around, this huge fight broke out after the rehearsal. Both sets of parents were about to call the whole thing off. The issue was the dowry. In Iran, the family of the groom would traditionally offer up a dowry: In case of death or divorce, the bride would be guaranteed to get a certain number of gold coins. Our parents had discussed the dowry months before, and they agreed that it was an outdated tradition.

But at the rehearsal dinner, a guest couldn't believe the bride's parents hadn't asked for a dowry. So they went to their daughter and told her she needed to demand a thousand gold coins—at $250 a coin. So she did. The bride told my brother they couldn't get married unless he agreed to it, he passed that message along to my parents, and everyone was upset. My parents felt that the dowry would set the marriage up for failure; it would put a price on the divorce. After four hours of yelling and crying into the wee hours of the wedding morning, everyone agreed that the American legal system would split the couple's assets in the event of a divorce.

The wedding day was still tense, and it was awkward being the only non–family member in the bridal suite. Then, as we were about to process, the sister insisted we change the order. It was originally supposed to go: sister, cousins, best friend, and then me. But she said, "Excuse me? You're not even family yet! You're not going last." And then every girl had an issue with where she was standing. Finally, I asked the officiant to line us up and I kept my spot at the end. I was so glad to spite the sister at that point.

In a Persian wedding, you sit on the ground in front of a place setting with a ton of things on it: honey for sweetness; eggs for fertility; coins for wealth; a prayer rug for faith; the "mirror of fate," in which the groom sees his bride once she sits beside him and removes her veil; and a bunch of pastries, cookies, herbs, and candies. We bridesmaids held a scarf over the couple's heads, and my aunt dusted sugar over the scarf to shower them in sweetness. We don't normally do vows or anything, but they did because that's what people do on TV.

The ceremony wasn't very religious, and neither was the reception: There was a cocktail hour, lots of dancing, and speeches. Of course the sister tried to give her speech before mine. But by the end of the day, the family tension had diminished. Now, a year later, things are okay between us—and most important, my brother and his wife are doing great.

—K, 28

THE NUN

IF YOU REALLY WANTED TO STRETCH the paradigm, you could say that all sisters have been bridesmaids. As I understand it, a bridesmaid is someone who supports her friend during a major moment. Sisters do the same thing with other sisters as they make vows. In both a wedding ceremony and a sister's vow ceremony, you are participating in this very hopeful thing, and the shared hope is that you can live up to what you are promising to do. You see the promise of a future that is better than it would be without a commitment to this other person. In our case, that other person is God.

The difference, however, is that a group of sisters makes their vows together—five or six of us might make a commitment to God at the same time. So, if you stretch the paradigm again, then the bridesmaids are also the brides. There are other differences too: My understanding is that a bridesmaid's job is to fix the train, make sure everyone arrives on time, and listen to way too many complaints. Although our ceremony is lovely—and we do get very excited about it—we are all just there to support one another and to contemplate the significance of the step we are about to take; there's less planning involved, and there are definitely fewer complaints.

I took my first vows in 1978, when I was twenty-one, with four other sisters. It seems silly to say, but I was both excited and nervous. Like any commitment, it was a leap in the dark. The five of us started planning our ceremony six months in advance. We had to pick the readings and the songs, and other elements of the mass. Like brides, we were thinking about the future: "Is this really the right thing? Is this a good fit?" It was helpful that I wasn't doing this alone, and I was lucky that the other sisters and I had a similar mind-set about what we wanted from our ceremony. There is this one song that makes my teeth hurt—it's hokey, and the melody is so trite that it reminds me of a circus tune—and everyone was fine with taking it off the table.

I have special connections with the "bridesmaids" whom I made my first vows with. We went through experiences that were deliberately formative, and we shared the challenges of going through all these new things. There will always be something special there.

We make our vows at the same point in a mass when a couple would exchange theirs. Then we leave the chapel, trade our white veils for black ones, and receive crucifixes. When we reappear before the laity, the difference in veil color isn't incredibly dramatic, but it's still a big difference. I've heard people gasp when they see it. It's a symbol of something—it brings faith into awareness.

For us, it's never love at first sight, never a quick romance and a Vegas wedding. Sisters take their first vows after a year of postulate and two years of novitiate—both of which involve reflecting and studying in a convent. I've heard it said that clergy are the last hopeless romantics on earth. You hear about people whose marriages didn't turn out well, people who struggled, and I am always shocked when they become cynical about love. I think sisters and priests have romantic notions above and beyond what people feel in a marriage, which is why I was sad to hear about some states enacting a class of marriage vows that are harder to get out of. If my fiancé said, "Honey, you're my sun, moon, and stars, but let's do the trial marriage," it'd take the wind out of my sails.

At a very, very, very basic level, the similarity between a sister's vow to God and a married couple's vows to each other is this: You have to take the idea of making a commitment very seriously. I don't think a vow of any kind should be a "let's see how this works" sort of thing. If that's your attitude, I know how it's going to work: not well. When married couples have talked to me about their relationships, I have a non-fairy-tale, feet-on-the-ground respect for the realities of that commitment. Everyone struggles, but I have sustained my commitment for thirty-five years—I know it can be done.

I remember talking to a friend who told me that the first year of marriage was the hardest. She was always taking her husband's perspective into account, and even though she had been living with him for years there was a shock of "Oh my god, he really does that?" and "Every Sunday at his mother's? You have got to be kidding me." She might have known those things before, but now they were a part of her life forever, which can be scary and is certainly challenging. One good thing about the convent is that we don't have to worry about in-laws! And that I won't ever live with the same group of nuns indefinitely. If my quirks bother you, fear not—this arrangement won't last forever.

—M, 56

THE JEWISH AMERICAN PRINCESS'S
BRIDESMAID

WHEN MY FRIEND REBECCA lost her mother when we were twenty-four, I was devastated. Rebecca and I grew up together, and her mother was a major presence in our Jewish community— she was a great family friend. So I remember feeling really upset and going to her shiva house all the time to just hang out and be there. A shiva is a weeklong open house where relatives and friends can mourn together.

One day, I was at the shiva house and our other friend Adina arrived. She sat down with Rebecca and me and she was immediately like, "Ohmygodohmygodohmygod, I just saw Levi walking in!" Levi and Adina had had this epic saga when we were in high school; they had dated on and off for three years. The shiva was a pretty somber affair, but Adina, who is naturally loud, just started JAPping out. She is your typical Jewish American Princess, the only girl in a family of three boys. We grew up in an affluent Jewish part of Long Island, and she was one of the most spoiled of all the pampered girls in our town. My earliest memory of her is from middle school. We were at the mall and she was talking to everyone at Limited Too because she went there so often. From then, it escalated—in high school she was all about "My mother got me this at Prada," and "Do you like my Gucci bag?" She's two years older than me, and frankly we became friends because she had a car and I didn't. She's a fun person to hang out with, and I love her, but she is a total JAP—very materialistic and self-involved.

Anyway, Adina left the shiva with Levi, and they ended up getting back together. They were engaged within a year. How did I learn they were getting married? She called me and—without a how are you or even a hello—yelled, "Guess. What. I'm engaged!" It was six years ago, but I remember it well—because she recently called to say, "Guess. What. I'm pregnant!"

My younger sister had gotten married a few months before Adina announced her engagement, and it was not a great experience for me. In our orthodox Jewish community, there's a lot of pressure to get married young, so when she got married at age twenty-two and I was twenty-five, everyone knew I felt stressed. But that didn't stop Adina from texting me five times a day about my sister's wedding: "Who did her makeup? Did she like her? Would she recommend the caterer? What about the flowers?" It was like pouring salt into my open wound. And then there was the constant discussion about Adina's dress: "I can't wait for you to see it," she said at least once a week for six months. "It's couture, but kind of modern. And kind of classic." In the end, the girl looked like she had been shoved into a cupcake—the dress was up to her neck, with long sleeves and a really fitted bodice and a poofy skirt. It was hardly flattering.

But Adina really surprised me by being a pretty low-key bride. Her bridesmaids, on the other hand, were even JAPpier than she was. When we were planning the shower, I had the idea of making Adina a DIY juice bar in my living room. She's a bigger girl, and she is always on these crazy diets. She has been on the cookie diet more times than I can count, and she's big into the juicing thing. The other bridesmaids were like, "Oh, I love that idea—let's order sushi platters, have a cake with her name on it, buy lingerie, and get her customized Victoria's Secret sweats." I vetoed all of it. I've been a bridesmaid thirteen times, and I've been generous to each bride, but I wasn't going to shell out hundreds of dollars on a shower. We just did the juice bar, and she loved it.

Adina's wedding was a big affair, but ridiculously disorganized. Plus, her uncle was a cantor, so I heard more prayer songs than I've ever experienced—just when you thought it was about to end, there'd be another high note. It was really painful. I was in heels and I thought I was going to pass out. The wedding started at 3:00 P.M., and we didn't eat until 8:00 P.M.

The whole thing made me realize that Adina and I were friends because of our history, not because we had anything in common. I just couldn't stand the friends she had made later on in her life. She was at my wedding a few years later, but we talk less now. We recently had dinner, and she wouldn't shut up about her Tiffany ring and her Louis Vuitton bag. And she still does this thing when she sees Rebecca that is both awful and funny. She says, "Oh, Rebecca, thank God for you. I wouldn't have ended up with Levi without you." Which is sort of like saying, "Thank God your mom died." And I totally know she doesn't mean that. But still: Oy.

—R, 31

THE GROOM'S EX-GIRLFRIEND

I DATED TONY FOR FOUR YEARS of high school and college, and when we broke up, we remained really good friends. It seems weird, but we were inseparable even before we started dating, so it felt natural to stay close.

Years later, Tony got together with his best friend's ex-girlfriend. I knew Sarah from when Tony and I dated: She's the kind of girl who puts on makeup to go to the corner store. She's blond and preppy; I'm a Jewish brunette. She just wasn't my scene. When Tony called me to tell me they were engaged, one of my first thoughts was that he would have to support her for the rest of his life. She was an aspiring actress, and she had already shown a propensity to spend ridiculous amounts of his money, pouring cash into Vineyard Vines–style stuff for the house they shared.

We went to his family's beach home in Maryland one weekend, and Sarah asked me to be in the wedding. Of course I said yes, but in the back of my mind I was thinking that I'd rather be on his side. I could only imagine all the things I'd have to do for her. I'd been a bridesmaid twice before, but both of those brides were really chill. Sarah, on the other hand, had already been saying things like "I need to look good in these pictures since it's my wedding year."

Sarah didn't have many friends, and she was pretty annoying during the "wedding year." They had two engagement parties, and she had us plan a bachelorette weekend away. I gritted my teeth for a lot of it. I remember my mom saying, "Do you think Sarah realizes that millions of people have gotten married before her?" She made us buy matching black shoes to go with our dresses, and they were so offensive I had to throw them away after the fact. And to top it all off, she chose to have the wedding at this colonial house in Virginia. It was a lovely setting, but a little odd because it had absolutely no significance to them. And everyone had to travel to get there.

She also made the wedding into this do-it-yourself situation even though she had a wedding planner and a big budget. The weekend of the wedding, I'd been driving for five hours, and the second I arrived, another bridesmaid rushed out to my car with a note instructing me to drop off gift bags at the guests' hotels. Sarah had actually written down tasks for us, so at various points throughout the weekend I'd get handed another piece of paper. Fine, I delivered the bags, but the duty made me wonder why she had forced me to book a room at the strangest B&B I had ever seen. All the other guests were in these sweet little places with friendly staffs, but the bridal party was in this weird house run by a guy with a lazy eye. Its greatest amenity was a creepy basement where they kept dusty old board games.

The day of the wedding—after we had paid to have our hair and makeup done—she gave me a paper that asked me to set up the chuppah. I'm not a rabbi, or even particularly religious—I thought it was a joke. It was 80 degrees outside, with 90 percent humidity. Once it was clear that she wasn't joking, I started panicking. I googled "What goes in a chuppah?" and began scavenging bits and pieces—a candle from a random dining table and a cup I saw laying around somewhere for the wine. I think it came together okay, but by the time the ceremony rolled around I was a sweaty mess. I was so distraught that I took a Xanax. It was one of the longest and hottest days of my life. I couldn't understand why she made her bridesmaids do these weird jobs while the wedding planner just stood by. I guess she liked being the center of attention.

I've never been so drunk at a wedding. By the time we got to the reception, I was over it—I was not going to dance and pose with the bridesmaids or any of that. We were wearing high-necked black dresses, so we looked like pilgrims wandering around this colonial house. I didn't have a boyfriend at the time, but I can genuinely say that I wasn't jealous of Sarah and Tony.

After all the pressure of the "wedding year," I was glad when it was over. Tony and I of course stayed in touch afterward, but I never became close with Sarah. They had been married for four years when Tony took me to lunch and said he had something to tell me. I thought she was pregnant, but it turns out she had been having a yearlong affair. I think I actually laughed when I heard the news because I was so nervous, and because the story was so insane and clichéd: He learned from an anonymous e-mail that she was sleeping with a tennis pro who had a wife and kids.

The divorce was not nice, and the whole thing is disturbing. I'm annoyed, too, that I spent so much time and money on a person who could hurt my closest friend. If anything, I learned that bridesmaids shouldn't feel such an insane sense of obligation leading up to a wedding. Like, would I have sweated so much over a chuppah if I had been able to predict the future? Um, definitely not.

—H, 32

THE LADY IN WHITE

LIKE MANY YOUNG WOMEN, I have dealt with the demands of your typical bridezilla—unique requests, expensive bachelorette parties, ugly dresses—so there wasn't that much that could faze me by the time I was in my childhood friend Jenny's wedding a few years ago. But then she told us that all of the bridesmaids would have to wear white. I think she was inspired by Kate Middleton, but it's a little different when you're getting married in Ocean City as opposed to Westminster Abbey.

I had lost touch with Jenny over the years, but we were each other's token friend from growing up: Of course I would be her bridesmaid, and of course I would do (almost) anything she asked. Her bridal craziness came on slowly, and it didn't really affect me until she solicited my advice on the bridesmaid dresses—and I learned that sometimes it's best not to be honest. When she asked what I thought about these gross, shiny white satin dresses, I said, "As a friend, I don't know if that's the best dress because it kind of looks stiff and cheap." Turns out she was already pretty set on the dresses, and she informed me that I'd be wearing it whether I liked it or not.

It was like having a white satin sheet wrapped around me. It looked like a strapless, floor-length toga—but it also looked like a wedding dress. When I tried it on, I legitimately looked like a bride. We bridesmaids were also going to wear these ugly necklaces that she had custom designed with her mom. I was like, "Oh my god! I love it!" Slash I'm never wearing this again.

Once we had chosen the dresses, the other bridesmaids started talking about going to SeaWorld for the bachelorette party. Jenny loves SeaWorld—she's obsessed with dolphins and killer whales and all that—and another one of the bridesmaids was also a twenty-eight-year-old who was obsessed with Sea-World. So weird. There was no way that I was spending a thousand dollars to go to SeaWorld, but I didn't want to be snobby or opinionated after the dress situation. So I did a cost analysis to show how expensive it would be, and defused the situation by suggesting some other places. We ended up going to Cape Cod and having a very tame time.

On the wedding day, we had to be at the hair salon at 7:30 A.M., even though the ceremony wasn't until 8:00 P.M. It was insane—we had three different photo shoots before the wedding even began. That morning, it seemed like Jenny started to realize that we'd all look like brides, so she decided that our hair needed to look different from hers. We were ordered to keep our hair down. It really cracked me up because I would look like a bride even if my hair was a greasy mess. People were congratulating me all day, and when I posted a picture of my boyfriend and me on Facebook, we got congratulatory comments from friends and family all over the world. We had only been dating for a couple of months, but my boyfriend was funny about it—he wanted to ask for cash gifts.

After six hours of photo shoots, the ceremony and reception were a blur. There wasn't anything memorable about the wedding other than that everyone was talking about all the ladies in white. But the bride was so happy, and she thought it looked perfect, which is all that matters—blah, blah, blah. I think you have to realize two things when you're a bridesmaid: 1. Don't give your opinion, no matter what, and 2. It's best to go with the flow and keep your sense of humor. Unless there's a SeaWorld scenario, because that just can't happen. No one is that good of a person, period.

—K, 30

THE "BAD" FRIEND

WHEN I WAS IN COLLEGE, I thought my five best friends and I would be like the Golden Girls when we grew up. I'm forty-three now, and we don't speak. And it's all because of a series of weddings, each of which went just a little bit wrong.

The first of us to get engaged was Karen, who was from this ritzy Boston suburb and who always wanted the white-picket-fence dream: the 2.5 kids, white dog sort of thing. She met a great guy and it was coming together for her. But her mom was so demanding, very Emily Post: She sent formal invitations and silver spoons to ask us to be in the wedding. When we went shopping for Karen's wedding dress, her mom asked why she couldn't be thin like me so she could wear cuter clothes.

A few months after Karen's engagement, our friend Jenna calls and says she's getting married too. There was always an undercurrent of competition within our group, but this topped everything: Jenna and her mother (also pushy, but less proper) hurried her planning and announced that her wedding would be a month before Karen's. The Internet wasn't huge back then—this was the mid-nineties—so I remember a flurry of calls: "Is she really doing this?" "I can't believe it!" Those conversations were pretty catty.

So Jenna's wedding was first, and Karen's mom walks into the ceremony with a pad of paper. She sits down in a pew and starts taking notes. You could imagine she was writing, "I would never do that," and "Nope, not doing this." She was shaking her head and occasionally sighing as she jotted things down. She brought the pad around with her all day—even taking notes at the cocktail hour and reception. We couldn't believe it. The ceremony was a huge Latin mass, and it was sweltering hot. We were wearing these long, heavy silk dresses with short jackets on top, and they were sapphire blue like Princess Diana's engagement ring.

Karen's wedding was different in that her Diana inspiration played out in the gown: It had big puffy sleeves and a big princess skirt with crystals. But nothing compared to our nineties hair: We all had such helmet head that mine didn't move for three days. My 'do was like a bigger version of "The Rachel." I look at the pictures and I can't believe anyone ever dated me with that hair. Karen's wedding was this very perfect event with ten bridesmaids and ten groomsmen. It was way too elaborate for me.

So when I got engaged two years after that, I decided on a small wedding with just one bridesmaid. I told my friends without thinking much of it, but a week later I got a call from Karen. She yelled at me for two hours about how I was a terrible, horrible friend. She said I had promised her the maid of honor position—referring to a drunken college conversation—as I apologized over and over again. I was completely blindsided. Who knows how many drunken promises I made in college? I never thought she'd react this way, and I was sure it would blow over.

A few weeks later, Jenna accidentally copied me on an e-mail to the group. She explained that everyone would need to cease being friends with me because I had betrayed the group by not asking everyone to be in my wedding. She said it was either her or me. Another of my friends replied to say "Of course we'll choose you." I don't think I had ever been so hurt; these were people I thought loved me no matter what. I wrote back and told them that I hadn't done anything wrong. I couldn't afford a big wedding with ten bridesmaids, but I still wanted everyone to be there for me.

They did show up to my wedding. They were polite and politically correct, and that was basically the last time I spoke to any of them. I went to a bachelorette party a few weeks later and Jenna got drunk and weepy and said she missed me as a friend. But I never heard from her after that.

There was a lot of heartbreak in the whole thing. In a way, it was like a mini-divorce. And to make matters worse, I was working at a bridal dress shop at the time, so I was surrounded by brides and bridesmaids every day. It was there that I realized that it's the mothers who are the real problem. The girls would come in so excited—they reminded me of Karen and Jenna— but their moms were trying to either relive their glory days or have total control. The number of girls who burst into tears in that store was crazy, and that's to say nothing of the catfights between the brides and their friends over bridesmaid dresses. That job was the most nightmarish experience of my life; I only lasted nine months.

In retrospect, I should have just asked the girls to be in the wedding. But I was stubborn, and when they made me seem evil, I got defensive. My first marriage ended in divorce, and the wedding severed such wonderful friendships that for my second marriage, I flew off to Puerto Rico. We got married on a beach with Red Stripes in hand.

—K, 43

THE CITY GIRL GONE COUNTRY

I GREW UP WITH SHELLY in a small town on the West Coast, and even though we kept in touch, we went separate ways. I got a degree in business, and she majored in nature studies at a school in Wyoming. A week before we graduated, I got this phone call: "I'm engaged, you're a bridesmaid, and you're coming to Wyoming for a week next summer."

So, at the age of twenty-three, I took a week off from my job at a Manhattan law firm, packed some kitschy Western wear—cowboy boots, jean shorts, the whole nine yards—and arrived in small-town Wyoming as directed, a week before the wedding. The town had one stoplight and one bar, and a population of women who, when they heard I lived in New York, kept asking me which *Sex and the City* character I was most like.

There were four other bridesmaids. One was the groom's sister, who was nineteen with a five-year-old daughter. There was a recent divorcée (age twenty-four), who thought she was a total expert on weddings and who was clearly on the prowl. My least favorite was my arch-nemesis from high school, who was so bitchy that she actually bumped me out of one of the photos on the wedding day. And then there was Shelly's sister, the peacemaker, who was the only sane one of us all.

All the bridesmaids and groomsmen were staying together in a sixteen-room cabin, and the plan was to do activities together every day. The idea of spending so much time with strangers reminded me of a reality TV show, especially given the motley crew of bridesmaids, but I was game—I had just broken up with my boyfriend of four years and I was coming from the single-guy wasteland that is Manhattan. Who knew there were so many young Sean Penn lookalikes hiding out in small-town Wyoming?

On the first night, I set my sights on this hot Wyomingan groomsman. Well actually, first I met a super-hot bartender. I asked the bride about him, and she was like, "You really are a New Yorker! He's the only gay guy in Wyoming!" Which was when I started talking to this groomsman who was like a *Brokeback Mountain*—esque cowboy, but not gay—I made sure of it. I felt a spark, but it turned out the divorcée thought she did too; she staked her claim right away. Many hours (and many whiskeys) later, after we had a big bonfire at the house, I realized I had left my boots somewhere near the fire. As I was searching for them, the cowboy came outside to help. We ended up kissing in the moonlight, and I was like, "This girl can hate me—I have to be with this guy." He had a cowboy swagger, like a strong, silent Marlboro Man. He drove a giant red truck and built log cabins for a living. It was almost too much. He was so hot.

For the rest of the week, he was basically my boyfriend. We went rafting, hiking, shooting, horseback riding, and kayaking, and he was by my side the whole time. He showed me the cabins he had built and drove me around in his big red truck. I'm used to New York guys who are like, "I'll call you when I call you," and here was this disarming gentleman. And he was smart too; not in the douchebag Wall Street way, but in the wilderness survival kind of way. I didn't sleep with him at first, because I'm not really like that, but then three nights in, we stayed out all night

under the stars in a grassy field by the cabin. I'm not going to go into details, but it was the best sex I've ever had. Ever.

The divorcée was pissed at first, but when more wedding guests came she was able to find someone else to be her rebound. During the wedding preparations, there was tons of weird competitive girl stuff: a constant battle over who would walk down the aisle first, a rivalry over who was the best flower-arranger—that sort of thing. I didn't really care, but my high school nemesis was the worst of all. Her claws really came out once she saw me with the cowboy, since she was jobless and single and lived at home with her parents. She was the kind of girl who got territorial about stuff like cake-baking—I mean, get a life.

On the morning of the wedding, we all got ready together. The bridesmaids were supposed to wear pink, and our dresses kind of matched our personalities. I'm outgoing and social, so I wore a nice paisley one-shoulder dress that was showy but not over the top. My high school nemesis wore this blah silk dress with thick straps and a run-of-the-mill cut, and the older sister wore exactly what the bride wanted: a pretty pink cotton dress. The divorcée was kind of a mess in this limp thing, and the teen mom showed up in a Charlotte Russe tube dress that was really tight and really short. The bride saw her and said, "I can see your vagina. Go change."

The wedding was held outside on a farm under this gorgeous pergola that the groom had built. It was beautiful and simple. The groomsmen wore Carhartt workpants and cowboy boots. I walked down the aisle with a guy named Christoph who worked on an oil rig—he was short and stocky and had this incredible Fu Manchu. I cried like a baby during the ceremony, occasionally making eyes at my cowboy and feeling like, "Oh my god, let's do this!" And then thinking, "Could I really?" And then trying to focus on my friend. It was weird standing there, watching my oldest friend getting married, and knowing that I could have the same nice life if I chose not to work crazy hours and live in a shoebox in New York.

After the ceremony, the married couple jumped onto a horse with a JUST MARRIED sign on the back of it, and took off through the field. And at the reception I realized that cowboys can really dance: They'll pick you up, spin you, and dip you—it was amazing. There was a country band followed by a jukebox, and I danced with my "boyfriend," the gay bartender, my dad, and of course the bride, who ripped off the sleeves of her wedding dress while yelling, "Fuck it, I'm married!"

I got caught up in the whirlwind of the whole thing, and I really thought about doing it: giving up my stressful, all-hours job and settling down with the cowboy in a log cabin he built with his bare hands. But I am intensely practical, and I have lots of things I want to accomplish before then. Still, whenever I have a crappy day at work or see photos of the bride's new baby, I think it might be a good idea to move out west. My friend and her husband are always asking me to visit, so maybe I'll do a trip out there—it wouldn't hurt to see how my cowboy is doing, either.

—F, 27

THE FASHION EDITOR

WHEN I WAS IN HIGH SCHOOL and college, my family and friends used to talk to me about clothes and style all the time. Now that I work in fashion in New York City, my sisters tell me they won't ask my opinion because they're afraid I'll say something harsh, and my friends seem scared to talk about anything clothing-related around me.

Every fashion editor feels that her personal taste reflects her work. Your look is a reflection of who you are and what you do in your job. I'm very specific about what I like—I only wear things that are minimal and modern. My uniform is a pair of leather pants or a cool-shaped skirt, and a simple shirt with some sort of architectural structure. I never wear heels; I usually do an oxford shoe that my boss says screams "chic lesbian." If I don't think something will work within those constraints, then I don't want it. And because I'm so selective, I think everyone else should be that way. Most people don't have a sense of direction, and I'm good at helping them find a style that they can stick to. I think if you don't wear something in a month then you should get rid of it. I'm that strict with myself.

I've been a bridesmaid eight times: for my sisters, and for friends from high school and college. They're all pretty classic

J. Crew girls, with a little bit of Anthropologie thrown in. They like bows and ribbons and they tend to be more trend-based than style-based. When I've been a bridesmaid, it's weird because what I'm wearing reflects the bride, not me; I feel like I lose my personality and take on a part of hers.

Like, my friend asked her bridesmaids to wear these black circle skirts with tan trim. There was nothing wrong with the skirt, but it was something that would look great on her—not me. She said we could choose any white shirt to wear with it, and any heel, which was both good and bad: I felt so out of my league that I didn't know how to handle it. At first I thought, "What would Jennifer wear?" and I considered wearing tights and a silk blouse tucked in with a belt (she's very conservative). That seemed crazy, so I went the other way and thought, "How could I make this skirt look cool?" When I asked my coworker what she thought about me wearing leather leggings under the skirt and putting a big boxy jacket on top, she laughed me out of her office. "You cannot wear leather leggings under a brides-maid dress!" she said, as if I should know such a thing.

It's not like I cared what people from home thought about how I looked, but my style is so tied into my idea of myself that departing from that feels funny. In the end, I wore a five-year-old trapeze-shaped shirt from Philip Lim's first collection, and I borrowed some Marni heels. I looked pretty frumpy-dumpy with this boxy shirt on top of the polyester skirt, and it was so weird for me to wear heels all night. Jennifer didn't say anything about my styling because she was obviously so wrapped up in all the excitement of the day, which made me think that I could have gotten away with the leather leggings.

I'm engaged. I want my dress to look exactly like this Céline dress from a few years ago that's crisp white silk, with a crewneck, a peplum waist, and a straight skirt that goes down to the floor.

It's minimal, modern, and sleek. I'm not having bridesmaids. If I think that people should each have a specific style, then why would I want to have a string of five people wearing the same dress? I'm so specific about what I like that if I were forced to have bridesmaids, I'd want them to wear something similar to my dress—and I'd end up standing at the altar surrounded by a bunch of mini-mes!

—A, 29

THE SEASONED PRO

I'VE BEEN IN TWELVE WEDDINGS in the past three years, and I've attended thirty-four weddings in the same time period. (I've been invited to forty-four.) I've spent $37,000—and I just turned thirty. Isn't that disgusting?

How do I even know so many brides and grooms? Well, I have five different friend groups—childhood friends, boarding-school friends, camp friends, college friends, and postgrad friends—and they all got married at around the same time. Also, I'm outgoing and enthusiastic, which I guess makes me an above-average wedding guest. I love a good party, but I hope people don't want me in their weddings just because I'm fun to have around. I think that each of the brides considers me a close friend—even if I don't consider myself quite as close with each of them.

Each wedding has been an unusual experience. The first time I was a bridesmaid, another bridesmaid got kicked out of the wedding. She got in a huge yelling-and-screaming fight with the bride at the bachelorette party, and they kicked each other out of their weddings (said bridesmaid was also engaged). I had to spend $450 on a dress that made me look incredibly fat. I would never ever have spent that much on a dress for myself. It made me so mad that right after the wedding, I threw it into a Dumpster at the hotel. I spent $1,400 on that wedding and I didn't even have to travel for it.

Then there was a wedding where a bridesmaid didn't fit into her dress. She didn't try it on after it was altered, and when she put it on in the bridal suite it just wouldn't zip. The bride was like, "Just leave and figure out how to fix it," as she sat getting her makeup done. Thankfully there was a pregnant bridesmaid who had an extra piece of fabric from her alterations. The mother of the bride cut the dress open and sewed a patch into the hip area. The bride was not happy. Later, the groom's brother spilled champagne all over me right before the photos were going to be taken. So I ended up in my underwear in the bathroom, sticking the dress under the hand dryer as other bridesmaids anxiously circled.

Oh, and there was the time that the bride's dress didn't fit the day before the wedding—it was just a little bit too tight. We spent the wedding morning thinking about what to do, and at last we had the bride lie down on her stomach while four of us shimmied the dress onto her and carefully zipped it up. We high-fived at the end and shouted, "Let's get married!"

At another wedding, a huge cat kept coming into the reception and I was charged with keeping him out. He was ginormous, like thirty-five pounds, and the bride kept freaking out and telling me to "get that fucking cat out of my cocktail hour." So I kept trying to carry the cat out of the building—it was a huge, huge cat—and he'd keep coming back. It happened at least ten times. Half of the pictures of me from the wedding show me carrying the cat. I finally gave up and started dancing with the cat.

What else? There were the weather disasters: One friend's wedding coincided with a big storm, so it was almost much smaller than she planned. A bachelorette party was canceled because of a hurricane, so I had to develop a contingency plan that would distract and satisfy the bride. I forced another friend to dress up like a Girl Scout and ask for badges at her bachelorette. One bride's mother-in-law called her fat the night before the wedding—as in, "You definitely didn't lose as much weight as you anticipated, did you?"—so I ended up sitting on the floor of the bathroom, trying to comfort my tearful friend. (Believe it or not, they actually have a great relationship now.)

So yeah, I've seen a lot. And I have the bridesmaid thing down to a science. When a friend calls to say she's engaged, I always send a ring holder. When she calls to ask me to be a bridesmaid, I'm always touched. When the maid of honor starts a group e-mail, and the bridesmaids throw out ideas for showers and bachelorette parties and gifts, I don't wait for someone to make a goddamn decision. I take charge.

First, I zero in on the girl in the bridal party who really wants a job. I can spot her from a mile away. She's Type A and crafty. You know she just wants to get construction paper and cut out "Congratulations!" or something. You need to give her a job or she'll never get off your back. So I usually task her with doing all the decorations for the shower and bachelorette party. Then, I kick the e-mail chain off with a message about the shower gift. If it's a small bridal party, I ask the girls to go in on a massage for the couple for their honeymoon. I swear, when I get married, I'll get so many couple's massages for my wedding that I'll have to do two a day. If it's a larger party, I'll ask every bridesmaid to give me sixty dollars, and I put together a bag full of beach stuff for the honeymoon. Everyone loves it. But if the bride has a sister, you have got to have her on your side. If she doesn't want to be involved then I go solo, because I don't want to be trapped in all the ideas on the e-mail chain.

This is the secret to being a good bride or bridesmaid: Do not ask for opinions. My favorite brides say, "Here's the dress, buy it by this day and wear shoes that are this color." My least favorite brides say, "Let's go to a bridal shop together and try on a million dresses so we can get one that looks good on everyone!" Read my lips: There's no such thing as a dress that looks good on everyone. It's sweet that you want to please the bridesmaids, but there's no point.

Before the wedding, I usually buy the couple a setting of the fine china on their registry. If the registry is picked over and it's a close friend, I buy Vera Wang frames and fill them with sentimental photos. If the couple is paying for the wedding, I give cash. On the wedding day, I stay out of the bride's way. No matter how chill she is, she's stressed out. I'm a loud, gregarious, talkative person, but I'm known for being silent on wedding days because I don't want to ruffle any feathers. And I know to stay away from the dress.

My boyfriend and I started dating at around wedding six, but the first wedding we attended together was wedding eight. That's a milestone for us. As a couple, we are popular at weddings— which means the bouquet has been tossed directly at me seven times. I always wanted to get married, and in the midst of all these weddings I happened to have met the person I think I'll marry. But I don't want to get married *because of* the weddings. In fact, the opposite might be true. I might have wanted an extravaganza of a wedding before, but now I want something incredibly simple. And no bridesmaids, of course.

—K, 30

THE JILTED EX

THE BEST THING about my breakup with Andrew was that I got to keep our mutual friends, Megan and Al. They took my side. When they got engaged, they asked me to be the maid of honor, while he was a lowly groomsman. I one-upped him there.

Megan and Al were the ones who set me up with Andrew, and we dated for almost a year. We were serious. He was talking long-term and whatnot. But then I went to France for a week for a wedding, and he Skyped me to say he didn't know if he wanted to be in a relationship because he wanted to focus on his business. I was somewhat hysterical, and I asked if we could talk about it in person. I got home on Sunday, and on Monday morning I got a businesslike e-mail from him, confirming his decision that we should break up. It included the sentence "Please call if you have any questions or concerns." I stupidly called him and told him off, and that was the last time we spoke.

I was pretty hooked on him, so the breakup was hard on me. I hadn't felt like that about a guy in a long time, and I never got closure because the last time I saw him we were really happy—smooching in the back of a carriage taking us through a snowy Central Park. Leading up to the wedding, I didn't want to worry Megan, or to let her know that I was freaking out about seeing him again. I didn't want to detract from her day in the slightest, so I'd ask really roundabout questions in order to get the scoop. I discerned that he had found a married woman to date a few months after he dumped me. Way to go for a whole lot more drama than I would have been.

The month before the wedding, I exercised every day and ate really well. I've never been so fit. I got a spray tan and eyelash extensions—but only partial ones, because I didn't want to look like I was trying too hard. I spent like three hours getting ready for the rehearsal dinner. I knew he and the married-woman girl-friend would be there. Of course he was the first person I saw when I walked in, so we had a weird hug and he introduced me to his girlfriend. She was wearing a black sparkly dress that stopped about a centimeter lower than her crotch.

Luckily, I was walking down the aisle with Al's brother. I had hoped to find a big hunk of a man to bring to the wedding, but that didn't work out. I did have a buffer date who was a good friend of the bride's, so he knew about the whole situation. After the ceremony, we spent a few hours driving around Chicago taking pictures, and Andrew and his girlfriend sat next to me and proceeded to make out for 90 percent of our time on the bus. Hunk or not, I was glad I had my date there.

My biggest saving grace was that I had only two glasses of wine that day. It took a great amount of self-control, but it was necessary to prevent mopeyness. And the wedding gave me the closure I needed. Celebrating Megan and Al's love made me re-alize that Andrew and I weren't right, especially given the way Andrew acted at the wedding. When you're in a relationship you look past so many things, so I never noticed how obnoxious he is whenever he meets new people, and that he does things like con-stantly refreshing his phone to check sports scores during his best friend's wedding. Plus, the fact that he would interfere with someone else's marriage made him way less attractive to me. When I saw him and his girlfriend sitting like sourpusses at the bar, I was glad we were over. And I was very glad I was sober.

I asked about him all the time before the wedding, but I let it go after I saw him. For some reason Megan recently told me that he and his girlfriend are talking about baby names—apparently he suggested my name and it prompted a big fight.

—A, 26

THE BIG SISTER

MY LITTLE SISTER had always been the sweetest, most accommodating person—until she got engaged at age twenty-four.

She was marrying a great guy who was just back from a fifteen-month tour of Iraq. They had a wonderful, beautiful romance—they love-cammed on Skype when he was serving—and they were two perfect peas in a pod who were destined to have beautiful, wide-eyed Gerber babies together. So when the spawn of Satan entered her, everyone was shocked.

This bridal poison started streaming through her blood and she demanded three showers, an engagement party, and the whole shebang. At first it wasn't so bad. While it was challenging for me to make the gift-wrap bouquet and write down all the gifts she got at her bridal showers—I'm deeply unartistic and easily distracted—I somehow made it through. And when I went with her to try on her wedding dress, it was easy to gush over her, saying things like, "Caitlin, you look so beautiful" over and over again.

But then I got an e-mail a couple weeks after. My sister said I wasn't taking her wedding seriously. That I didn't even say anything when I saw her in the wedding dress, and that I wrote down "wineglasses" instead of "wine decanter" when I made the gift list at the bridal shower. Did I *know* how embarrassing it would have been for her to send the wrong thank-you note?

Oh my god. First off, how hard did she want me to gush? And second, no one had any idea what they got her because it was all off her registry! But that's not how I replied, of course. I said that I was so sorry she felt that way, and of course I cared about her wedding. For a year, this sort of snappy-and-sycophantic back-and-forth was the norm. I'd tell her about a part of the bachelorette party I was planning or about an idea I had for one of the showers, and she'd reply with pure snark. She was constantly accusing me of not caring. Instead of being like, "What the hell are you talking about?" I'd try to mollify the little monster with things like, "I appreciate you saying something. I'm so supportive of you. I'm your number one fan." I talked her off a ledge and never told her she was a psycho, but inside I was exploding.

What was hard was that Caitlin is not a heinous person—she's funny and delightful. And although we fought like crazy growing up, I had always been able to look at her in a certain way and make her laugh, and the spat would be over in an instant. But in the months leading up to the wedding, I completely lost that ability. I think she was really afraid of the huge life change, and that this was at the root of her attitude. The only thing she didn't do was accuse me of being jealous, thank God—because maybe I *was* jealous that her husband was coming between us. I had always been her protector, and now I was giving up that responsibility. But the main thing was that I wanted her to stop hating me. How could I convince her that I gave a shit?

On the wedding day, I just wanted to stay the fuck away from her but instead I gave an awesome speech. I played the role and gave her a hug. You'd never know there was tension. But there was.

We didn't speak for a year. My mom finally sat us down and made us talk things through. Everyone cried. She thought I didn't make her a priority, and I thought I'd never live up to her expectations of the perfect bridesmaid. Life is about managing peoples' expectations, so maybe brides could set the bar a little lower. I understand that bridesmaids could be more accommodating, but maybe brides could also start being more considerate of peoples' time. Tell me you're going dress shopping on Saturday, and let me decide if I want to go.

—A, 30

THE BRITISH LADETTE

ALEX IS MY CLOSEST FRIEND in the world. We met when we were eighteen and she was fond of this terrible, pink, fluffy mohair sweater. From then on, we were inseparable. I went out with her brother for two years, and after college we lived together in the slowly gentrifying projects in East London. We were on the tenth floor of a twenty-story council estate. Someone had written in its stairwell: "Do not shite in the stairwell. If you do, I will kill you."

Alex is very low key, but very stylish. She's everyone's worst nightmare: incredibly sporty, very bright, hilariously funny, attractive, and no-fuss too. Take her wedding, for example. I had wedding-dress shopped with so many friends and seen them agonize and spend thousands of dollars. But she found a simple, heavy silk dress she liked on J. Crew's Web site and bought it on eBay for a hundred dollars. She had it shipped to me because I was living in New York at the time, and I brought it back to London on a visit home. She tried it on in the loo of the bar where we were having drinks and just came out and said, "That'll do." It was really cool. And of course she looked gorgeous in it.

Naturally, I had to plan her hen party, which is what English people call a bachelorette. It started in the afternoon in a park in

London, where we drank prosecco and had a sports day. We did egg-and-spoon races and a three-legged race, and I had pasted her fiancé's head on a lifesize cutout of a naked man so we could play pin-the-penis-on-Bill. I had baked breast cupcakes, with pink frosting and a pink nipple in the middle, which were a big hit. Alex was thirty-two when she got married, and lots of her friends were new mothers. We were drinking quite heavily, so they were all pumping and dumping their breast milk, which Alex found very strange. She had this odd antipathy toward breastfeeding.

Every hen will tell you "Don't dress me up," but one has to know to ignore that. So we put learner license plates around her neck, strung streamers in her hair, crowned her with a tiara covered in blinking lights, and made her drink from penis-shaped straws. In some ways, Alex is quite extroverted, but she can also be quite shy—so it was her worst nightmare to be dressed up like an idiot bride.

After a few hours of games, we stumbled into a pub at the edge of the park. As I say, Alex was slightly squeamish about breastfeeding. So when our friend Camilla had to run to the bathroom to use one of those ridiculous breast-pump contraptions, we came up with a fantastic idea. We made Alex a very special shot: Kahlúa, Baileys—and breast milk. She took it and thought nothing more of it, and we didn't tell her about its special ingredient . . . until the wedding day.

The wedding was held at a mutual friend's Georgian estate in the north of England. Alex and Bill were on a budget, but they did things so stylishly—it was all roses in little old bottles and that sort of thing. We processed down a grand staircase, and although the ceremony was short, it was also incredibly moving. Alex's mom wrote a very good poem, and there were quite a few tears.

Then came the speeches. Generally, in England, only the men make speeches. The father of the bride goes first, then the groom, and then the best man. The best man's speech is meant to rip the piss out of the groom, and this couple's past was filled with so much mad twentysomething behavior that there was plenty of material. Alex and I have always thought it was sexist that not a single woman speaks at your average wedding, so she and I were going to say something as well. Alex gave a funny and eloquent speech, and then I was up.

Having known Alex for fifteen years, I had a lot to say. And the breast-milk incident was too funny not to include. I tested it on my mom, who is quite straight, and she thought it was hilarious. I wasn't sure if it was too controversial, but I was only really concerned about whether or not Alex would be offended. I knew she'd have a laugh about it, so I went for it.

I think the line was something like, "We all became a bit closer at Alex's hen night, but she didn't quite realize the extent of it. You know that shot we gave you? It was milky, right? Well that wasn't cow's milk." The room was divided into people who laughed and those who stared at me in shock. Generally, the people with babies were horrified, and those who didn't have them were less horrified, but it wasn't an even split because Camilla had provided the milk, after all, and she had a child. I also expect that some people had no idea what I was on about. Thankfully, Alex thought it was funny. Later, there were a lot of "Ughh, Camilla, how could you?" and some suggestion that the substance I had alluded to was actually semen. That literally hadn't occurred to me.

I was so relieved to have the speech out of the way that I downed a couple of champagnes and thought no more of it. I'm sure some thought to themselves, "Who *are* these people?" but I wasn't particularly ostracized. I forgot all about it in order to have a snog with the man who owned the house. I was wearing a green dress, so we were henceforth referred to as "the country gent and the lettuce." As in, "The country gent has his hands on the lettuce."

Alex has two children now, and while I have found that children often change friendships, ours hasn't changed in the slightest; we are still extremely close. Plus, I like to think that—having forced her to inadvertently drink her best friend's breast milk—I cured her of her squeamishness and allowed her to feed her firstborn.

—L, 35

THE GAY BRIDESDUDE

THE BEST PART about my friend Nan's wedding was the bachelorette party in Miami. I was the only guy in a group of eight
girls, and when we went to a nightclub, the bouncer pulled me
aside and asked me, "How did you pull all these ladies?" It was
the best weekend of my life! For the first time in my life, I had
swagger. And the girls humored me—they didn't tell anyone it
was a bachelorette party and pretended that I was a total bro.

Nan is one of my closest friends—so close that she didn't even
have to ask me to be in the wedding. When it came time she said,
"You're going to be in the wedding party, right?" It was totally
natural. When she first started dating her husband I remember
he was always trying to impress me, which I appreciated. They
were long distance for most of their relationship; he lived in New
York and she lived in Chicago. But he'd often come to Chicago
for conferences and to visit friends, so they saw quite a bit of
each other. But after a few months of this, I got a text from Nan
saying that Mahesh was a big liar. I freaked out and called her
right away. She told me that he had made the whole thing up just
to have an excuse to come see her. And that's when we knew he
was the one.

It was a traditional Indian wedding: The ceremony, which was in Sanskrit, was three hours long and hugely religious. They gave each other necklaces, they had to eat certain things, and the priest gave them lots of blessings. At one point a groomsman and I had to go up on stage and participate. So it was me—a gay Jewish guy—and a Muslim groomsman up there with this Indian couple; it was like a United Colors of Benetton ad. We took off our shoes and walked around a fire pit three times in one direction. I'm not sure what the significance was because honestly, I was starving. The wedding was so long that they actually served hors d'oeuvres during the ceremony, and I would have eaten some if I had known it was going to go on like this—all the Indian families were doing it.

I was one of four male bridesmaids, and I was the only gay guy. It wouldn't have made sense for us to be groomsmen because we were much closer to Nan. So the four of us were called "bridesdudes." We wore kurtas that matched the bridesmaids' saris, which were cornflower blue and yellow. There were about five hundred people in attendance, which is why it was held in New York even though Nan and Mahesh were living in Chicago. New York's Gotham Hall was the only large enough venue they could find on such short notice: According to Hinduism, they needed to get married on an auspicious date determined by their priest, and that day happened to be only three months after their engagement.

The bride and groom's first dance was a mash-up of Bollywood dance moves and American ones, the food was Indian-but-American—creamy curried sauces with chicken and puff pastry—and the booze was hidden behind a curtain in an anteroom out of respect for the older Indian contingent. The exoticism of it all was cool, but my favorite part—other than my baller bachelorette-party status—was getting to know Nan's friends. I didn't think that Nan and I could get closer, but now I feel even more engaged in both her new and old lives—like I understand her in a different way.

—Z, 30

THE SECRET-KEEPER

WHEN MY FRIEND LAUREN'S job got transferred to Southern California, she and her boyfriend did long distance between there and Seattle. He visited her a week after she left, and he came home with an STD. He called Lauren and said, "You gave me herpes! I'm never talking to you again." She denied it up and down. She said that *he* had cheated on *her* if he had an STD, because she was clean. We were all pretty sure she was guilty though. He was a nice guy—I felt bad for him.

Lauren is a loyal person—to her friends at least. We've known each other since high school, and she's one of those take-it-or-leave-it sorts of people: Yes, she was shady and something of a pathological liar, but if you just accepted that then you could appreciate her thoughtfulness and sense of humor. But she always had a boyfriend, and her boyfriend always defined her. So it wasn't totally surprising to me when she met another guy a few weeks after the breakup—or when they moved in together just a month after they had met.

They were engaged shortly after, and she asked me to be a bridesmaid. She wasn't a nightmare bride at all; she just told us what dress to buy (it made me look horrible, but that was to be expected), and she said she wanted to go to a strip club for her bachelorette party. So we went to a really seedy place where half-naked guys try to pin you up against a wall and dry-hump you. She loved it because she's really outgoing and petite—the guys were picking her up and straddling her, and she was playing right into it. She got up on the stage with them and everything. I wasn't surprised that she wanted to do that, or that she enjoyed it so much. She was the bride, so whatever floated her boat!

The groom was a great guy who let her wear the pants in the relationship. It was almost like he was afraid of her. They were living in California, and all of Lauren's bridesmaids were living in Seattle, so we didn't know him very well, although one of the bridesmaids, Kate, made more of an effort than the rest of us. The groom called Kate a month or two before the wedding to tell her that he was having second thoughts about the whole thing. He seriously spilled, telling her that he had gotten herpes from Lauren and that he felt sort of trapped by the fact that they had the same STD. He wondered if he'd meet someone else who'd accept that. He said he had spoken to his sister about it, and that she had found him a dating Web site for people with STDs.

It was such a strange situation. Kate was obviously loyal to the bride, but she also didn't want to coax the groom into the wedding if it wasn't right. It's hard to see having an STD in common with someone as a good reason to get married! And then we also all knew for sure that Lauren had lied about the whole herpes thing. Gosh, it was like a soap opera. So Kate tried to advise the groom not to worry about money or short-term adversities, but to really think about what he wanted and to talk to Lauren. He did end up doing that, but Lauren told him it was too late for that kind of talk: They had to go through with it because her parents had spent so much on the wedding.

We jokingly wondered whether he'd be a runaway groom, but he was definitely too scared to do that. In retrospect, the terrible thing is that we never told Lauren about all this backstory. It just seemed like she wanted to put on a happy face and get on with it. We didn't want to confront her with the herpes stuff so we just let her keep up the charade.

The wedding was lavish and cheesy—chocolate fountain, ice luge, that sort of thing—and sometime afterward, Lauren and I lost touch. I don't know how it happened; I think she lied about something and fought with another bridesmaid, and suddenly she had blocked some of the bridesmaids on Facebook. I was still her friend (on Facebook at least), so everyone would look at her pictures from my phone, but one day I noticed that I had been defriended. I did text her once or twice to try to fix things, but I wasn't even sure I wanted to be her friend (on Facebook or otherwise): As interesting as it was, I didn't want to get pulled back into all her drama.

We bridesmaids heard that Lauren got divorced about two years after the wedding, and a couple months ago I started thinking about getting back in touch with her. I felt guilty. But then I looked her up on Facebook and I saw that she's engaged again—and she's having a whole new set of six bridesmaids. All these scary thoughts went through my head about what could potentially happen if I wrote her a note: What if she invited me to the wedding, and I had to get her another gift? Or even worse: What if she asked me to be a bridesmaid again? I quickly logged off and ditched the idea. Maybe after the wedding I'll give it another go.

—P, 30

THE BURNING MAN BRIDESMAID

TOM AND I MET AT BURNING MAN IN 2003. Burning Man is a weeklong camping experience in the Nevada desert, and it's all about intuition and experimentation—and hallucinogens. It was my second time at the festival, but now I've been eleven times.

We were playing a giant game of pick-up sticks: Instead of straws and rubber balls, there were PVC pipes and beach balls. I was dressed like a fairy, and this guy was like, "You have to meet my friend Tom—he loves fairies." So I invited them to a "fairy formal" we were having that night. The second Tom walked in, we stared straight at each other and I thought, "I really like that guy. He's a really good person." From then, I was smitten.

We met at Burning Man again the next year, and the year after that and the year after that; the third year was the one where he told me that he was in love with me. But I had just started dating this guy, so the timing was off. He said the funniest thing—that he felt comfortable just loving me and receiving nothing in return. He described his feelings as a very free, open love that feels good just expressing itself: a love that doesn't need to be acted on. I was comfortable having it be a friendship. I didn't feel like it needed to go anywhere special for me.

When Tom e-mailed before the next year's Burning Man to

say that he was dating someone, I knew this girl had to be amazing. And from the moment Mary and I met, we really got along. Sometimes, when you meet a guy friend's girlfriend, there's a competition or uncertainty there, and Tom is so adored on the playa (which is what the Burning Man grounds are called) that you'd think there'd be an element of that. But she was totally nonchalant—completely easygoing and fluid—and our conversation went back and forth like lightning.

A couple of months later, she threw Tom a big fortieth birthday party and she invited me to fly out to New York City as a surprise guest. She also told me, "Hey, look, if you want to hook up with Tom over the weekend, by all means—you're more than welcome to." So I flew out and I spent a few great days with them, the three of us sleeping together in a burrito of a bed. But there has never been a sexual attraction between Mary and me, and Tom and I didn't hook up that weekend.

In fact, the only time we've ever hooked up was the day before his wedding. That was a year later, at Burning Man, and we were making out one afternoon behind a DJ booth. Mary was there too. We had kissed before, but this time there was a spark for some reason. It occurred to me that it might be fun to have sex right then and there. So I stopped making out with him for a minute and turned to Mary and said, "Hey, do you mind if I have sex with Tom?" And she was like, "Sure, that's totally fine." They're part of a Burning Man camp that's very pro-polyamory, and their relationship was open. He was grabbing my ass and kissing me, so we ended up having sex right there in front of a dozen or so people. Later, Mary told me it was one of the most profound experiences of her life—seeing her future husband with someone else without feeling jealousy or resentment. And I felt the same way. I wouldn't have suggested it if I thought it'd be weird. It was sort of like asking, "Hey, can I have that sandwich?" And she was like, "Oh, totally, no big deal."

The next day was the wedding, and they told me to come to the temple, which is a beautiful raw-plywood construction that people write all over with Sharpies to commemorate friends and family members who have died, or things that are important to them. I biked out there and realized that they were all waiting for me to start the ceremony, which surprised me: I didn't think I was essential to the event. But I guess I was the only bridesmaid, and I ended up wearing almost exactly the same outfit as the bride: a corset, a tutu, and goggles, with braided hair. The rest of the guests were crazily dressed: One girl was wearing a fur jacket with nothing underneath, and there were a bunch of people dressed in samurai costumes.

Everyone stood around them in a circle, and we read passages that had been written by their families, who couldn't (or wouldn't) make it to Burning Man. Weddings here are more free-form than traditional ceremonies. The dad doesn't give the bride away, there's no aisle to walk down, and I doubt that Tom and Mary would be the types to use the words "husband" and "wife." As they were saying their vows, they took a moment to recognize the role I had played in their relationship. They said that I was a member of their marriage, and that, in a sense, the three of us were getting married. I was really surprised and flattered. It blew my mind.

Afterward, we went back to camp, where our friend had custom brewed his own moonshine ginger beer. We planned on going out, but it was such an emotional day that we were exhausted. So a bunch of us, including the newlyweds, fell asleep in our yurt in one big cuddle puddle.

I have been in love once before, when I was much younger,

but Tom and Mary give me an idea of what it would be like if I found love again. They have that combination of great big feelings and the normal, everyday aspect of being with someone. If I ever get married, I'd want to have as meaningful a ceremony as they had. But I honestly don't know if I could handle an open relationship. I've always been amazed by Mary's openness and maturity, and I really struggle with monogamy: Do I want it because society shows us images of it all the time, or do I want it because I want it—because I couldn't stand my partner being with someone else? I guess polyamory would be fine if I felt really strongly and my partner felt the same way—if we had a love that was as strong as Mary and Tom's.

—L, 31

THE ANTI-BRIDESMAID

I HAVE NEVER BEEN A BRIDESMAID because I'm not a big proponent of marriage. I just don't plan on getting married. Ever.

I have a serious issue with same-sex couples being forbidden from marrying. In fifty years' time—or hopefully before then—we will look back on the inability of gay folks to marry like we remember slavery. The people who coexisted with slavery without doing anything weren't as culpable as those who encouraged it, but they were still at fault. The same goes for heterosexual couples who are for same-sex marriage but still participate in the institution. They're complacent; they're turning a blind eye.

I don't want to be heard as disparaging or homogenizing heterosexual folks who marry. If you are entering a religious institution—an agreement with God—then that makes sense. In fact, there's a whole bunch of good reasons to get married: You might need to stay in the country, or you might need to be on your partner's health insurance. But other than that, I've never needed the state to structure my personal relationships. Relationships come in many forms, but when marriage is forced to fit into a mold by law—when it's forced to be structured a certain way—it's not right.

I was in a relationship with a man for a decade, and we

consciously decided not to get married. My parents and friends thought that he and I hadn't crossed that bridge yet—that we weren't serious—but we were in a conscious, committed, consensual, and loving relationship with all the trappings of marriage. Just not the legal ones. It was beautiful and wonderful, and the fact that we weren't married contributed to its beauty. We stayed not because it'd be messy to leave, but because we loved each other. It ended beautifully and wonderfully as well because we didn't have to legally undo the relationship. Extracting ourselves from each other emotionally was difficult enough; I think we're both better people because we didn't have to extract ourselves legally.

My sister is getting married in a couple of months, and I am planning on going to the wedding. I would have been put in a precarious position had she asked me to be a bridesmaid, but she didn't; she knows and respects my beliefs on the whole situation. She appreciates me just being there because I don't go to weddings often; I have only been to one, and I'm in my thirties.

Being a bridesmaid could be a beautiful testament to love. It's probably sweet to have your closest friends stand next to you as you promise your partner that you'll love him forever. But when I think about the number of female friends that I really trust— and who would be genuinely happy for me if I got married—it's so small. If I got married today in an alternate universe, I can think of one person I trust like that. If you're lucky enough to find one person whom you can spend the rest of your life with, you're even luckier if you also find one female friend who truly loves you.

But that's not what being a bridesmaid seems to be about. I love watching the show *Bridezillas,* and what I gather from it is that some brides don't want to be surrounded by people they love; they just want to be envied. A lot of times, the bridesmaids' function is to make the bride feel more special—to feed her ego. If my one best friend wanted me to be a bridesmaid in her wedding, I would want to do something different with the role. I'd want to be the fantasy version of a bridesmaid—the girl who's able to observe a happy time in a friend's life, and to be genuinely glad for her.

—A, 35

THE CALAMITOUS JANE

THE FIRST CRISIS of my stepsister Tracy's wedding day occurred when we were getting ready to sign the *ketubah*. It's the official marriage license at Jewish weddings. It was nowhere to be found. My mom had to rush home and grab it, but she couldn't find it at our house either; turns out it was at Tracy's mom's house, so she had to drive there and then back to the wedding. We started an hour behind.

I was eighteen and a freshman in college, and I was petrified of gaining the Freshman Fifteen. Plus, hello, I wanted to look good in my bridesmaid dress! So I had developed this habit of not eating a lot. I'd snack rather than eat big meals. But that day, there wasn't much food around, so once we had finally signed the *kehtubah*, I had nothing in my stomach when I processed down the aisle. It was February, and I had just come from freezing-cold New York to Nashville, which was record-settingly hot that year. That day, it was eighty degrees. And it was an outdoor wedding.

So you can see why I fainted. I saw myself as a young hotshot, coming home from college wearing heels. But, as I had been told, standing on the grass in those heels was a little silly. I started to feel dizzy, and I whispered to my sister-in-law, who was next to me, that I felt like I was going to faint. She hissed,

"Don't lock your knees," but my knees were already bent. I said, "I'm going down." And I did. Luckily, there was a row of empty chairs behind us, so I scooted out of line and blacked out on my way to the chair. I have to say that it was really well done; I completely avoided commotion. Someone brought me water, and I mumbled, "Don't tell Tracy—don't tell anyone." I was feeling fine by the time we recessed at the end, and I had gotten off scot free because Tracy didn't know I had fainted. But I also felt sort of guilty, like I needed to redeem myself as a bridesmaid.

There was another long pause before anyone ate. We had to take pictures and all that. My dad is diabetic, and he too hadn't eaten all day, even with the hour-long wait for the *kehtubah*. So when we finally sat down to dinner, he was so hungry that he started eating way too fast. He was digging into this food—I think it was steak—and then he stopped midbite and got this look on his face. Once my family saw that look, we all knew what was coming: He was about to vomit everywhere.

This is a weird thing that he does. He's always hungry, and he takes big bites and forgets to chew them, and then he throws up. So once he got the look on his face I knew to try to shield the table and my mom knew to try to get him out the door. He stood up and started to gurgle a little, and then it all started to come out. I looked up at him, then down at my other sister, Emily, and I saw him vomit on her shoulder. She craned her neck around to look at the puke, and her face unquestionably said, "Are you fucking kidding me?" I'm not joking when I say there was this moment of silence before all the shit blew up. I grabbed my sister and scooted her to the bathroom, managing to push her through the door before she burst into tears. I shoved her in a stall just as Tracy came in. "What's going on? Is everything okay?" she asked, concerned-slash-suspicious. "Yeah, great, happy, wedding, awesome, awesome," was my reply. She left, probably unconvinced, and I started to work on cleaning Emily's shoulder. The vomit wasn't chunky, and her dress was cotton, so it was pretty easy to clean.

When we returned to the reception area, I saw my aunt spill a glass of red wine all over our table. I followed her eye line and realized I hadn't really covered up what was happening. The room had glass walls, and everyone could see my dad puking in the bushes outside, including the bride. She was very cool about it—and aside from all that, the wedding was pretty drama-free.

—N, 26

THE LESBIAN'S BRIDESMAID

IN THE PAST TWO YEARS, I've been a bridesmaid in three weddings. What none of the brides know is that I'm secretly married.

The thing is, I've never cared about getting married. I was never the little girl making grand plans for her wedding; I've never liked being the center of attention. And so when my boyfriend of six years got offered a two-year job rotation in Italy—and I learned that we'd have to be married if I wanted to go with him—I didn't want to take on the whole stressful wedding issue. So we got married in secret at a courthouse. And although the friends we made in Europe knew we were married, none of our American friends or family know about it to this day.

When I was abroad, my very best friend in the world, Helen, got engaged and started planning her big ol' lesbian wedding to Whitney, her girlfriend of a few years. It was hard for me to help much from Italy, so my only task was to purchase all the gimmicky party favors for her bachelorette party. I wanted something ridiculous. What I had in mind was a giant six-foot inflatable vagina, but there were no inflatable labia to be had online. So I settled for a bunch of vagina straws and a Japanese anime blow-up doll with three "love tunnels." It was really appalling. And also incredibly funny. I ordered it with my husband's credit card, because that's what we used for American purchases, and I had it shipped to another bridesmaid, who was living in San Francisco.

A few weeks later, my husband got a cryptic text from his mom: "Something came in the mail for you and I'm really confused." He called her, and I started putting it all together while they talked on the phone. The package had been sent to the credit card's billing address rather than the shipping address, so my husband's mom opened the box and found the doll in a box covered in photos of barely clothed Harajuku girls fondling themselves in an absurdly lewd way. And of course it was addressed to me.

His mom responded fairly well to the fact that her potential daughter-in-law (well, real daughter-in-law, but she doesn't know that) had sent her pornographic materials. She is really traditional, and she doesn't like me much, but she seemed to think it was cool that I had a lesbian friend who was getting married. I e-mailed her saying, "So sorry you received the package, but I really need that stuff!" She was a complete sport about shipping it to the other bridesmaid. I was receiving these little e-mails from her like, "There was a free gift in the box—the Chick Licks gum! I forgot to send it but I'll put it in the mail today." I mean, I saw myself as being in good standing with his parents, but every time I think of this incident I just see my stature falling and falling and falling.

The bachelorette party was hysterical. When we first started planning we thought maybe the two brides would have their parties together, since they're both girls. But Helen was like, "Uhhh, no. Why would we do it together?" She's a party animal and Whitney is quieter, so Whitney had a casual weekend away with a few friends, and we had a very boozy, crazy time. There was a great debate over whether to have a male or female strip-per, because all the bridesmaids were straight. Helen thought a male stripper would be better for everyone, but in the end we were totally terrified—after all, it's a guy's groin in your face.

Helen and Whitney both had personal trauma leading up to the wedding. Helen's fundamentalist aunts and uncles wrote the most hurtful letters you can imagine to her parents when they received the invite, and Helen's dad—a quiet guy who has grap-pled with Helen's sexuality quite a bit—wrote back saying that he no longer considered them to be a part of his family. Whit-ney's dad had made a point of ignoring her sexuality, and he wasn't sure if he could walk her down the aisle. But in the end he did, and he gave an amazing speech in praise of their relation-ship. It was a huge moment for her, and a highlight of the night.

The wedding was so, so beautiful. It was at this lodge in Northern California. Totally idyllic. There were some meltdowns about seating arrangements and last-minute minutiae, and then there was this former newscaster doing our makeup whose top Google Image result was a mug shot. Turns out she had attacked her boyfriend's mistress. She was actually pretty great.

Both of the brides wore really girly, froufrou dresses, and they had a bluegrass band accompany them down the aisle. I think giving the speech at Helen's wedding was one of the top five proudest moments of my life. You know when you just nail something? I feel really close to her family and friends, and it was such an amazing and incredible privilege to communicate what she means to me with everyone she holds dear.

I loved being there for my friend and helping her realize her vision. But it made me feel more strongly than ever about not doing something grandiose if I ever make my marriage more of-ficial. Helen is nontraditional like me, so I asked her what made her decide to have a big wedding. Her first response was "I have no idea," but then she posited that there was no other open forum for her and Whitney to show their commitment to each other.

It's funny because in Europe, I hated the loaded connotations that came with being a "wife." That label turned me into a boring old hag. But in the United States, where I'm a "girlfriend," people are constantly asking when I'm getting engaged. And I'm equally resentful of this—of the expectation that marriage is always the logical next step. For me, wanting security or affirmation is the most terrifying reason to get married. But I'm all for a party or a big open bar when I'm ready, because only at weddings and funerals do you get to have everyone you like in one place. Plus I really like small appliances, and it seems like weddings are great for that.

—B, 28

THE VIRGIN

MY BROTHER GOT ENGAGED when I was seventeen, and his fiancée asked me to be her maid of honor. I was thrilled. It was a very important time for me socially at high school—I was becoming kind of cool as a junior, but I was still dorky at heart. The wedding was just weeks after I had sipped my first alcoholic beverage (a Mike's Hard Lemonade), and I was trying hard to develop a smoking habit even though I got sick every time I took a drag.

My big goal for the wedding was to give a great speech. I was very close to my brother, and I loved his fiancée; I wanted to do them proud. I studied the greatest speechwriters of our time, I got a book on writing the perfect toast, and I prepared this ridiculous rhyming poem that I practiced over and over again. I was of course wearing a terrible dress—highlighter yellow, with a boatneck and this crystal belt. I also had an updo and too much makeup, which at the time felt super sexy. When I conjure the whole look now I think, "Oy yoy yoy."

My second goal was to not let my parents see me sneaking drinks from the open bar. It was the most exciting thing, and no one really paid attention to me until I tipsily went outside to smoke a cigarette and I accidentally put it out in the chest of my dress. My mom saw it and said, "No more champagne for you, young lady!" and I was like, "Okay, mom," before continuing to get drunk.

And my third goal materialized as I walked into the cocktail hour, when I set eyes on the piano player. He was my sort of dreamboat: glasses, brown hair, dorky vibe. I was all innocently like, "Mom, who's he?" and she said he was a friend of my brother's—a sophomore in the music school at USC. We eye-flirted for the entire cocktail hour, and after my speech was a total success (I got through it without hiccuping; everybody laughed), he came up to me and we started talking.

By the end of the wedding, he was playing me ballads on the piano. I remember sitting beside him on the bench as he played "Lush Life." I thought it had to be a really romantic song and I always requested it after that—until I realized it's about two alcoholics trapped in a downward spiral. Anyway, it seemed perfect then, and I was besotted with the pianist by the time we joined everyone at a nearby bar. It was a shithole college pub, and when we got there, we started making out. Most of my family wasn't there, thankfully, but some of my aunts and uncles were probably like, "Megan is really coming out of her shell, huh?"

I brought him back to my room in the wedding hotel, which was risky because my parents were staying next door. I proceeded to lose my virginity to him. I didn't tell him that of course, but I bled everywhere. He was like, "Um?" and I was like, "Gah!" It was only then that my age came up, but I persuaded him that I was an old soul with statements such as: "I don't listen to Britney Spears in my car; I listen to Miles Davis."

I couldn't have planned it better. I had dated someone at high school whom I didn't want to sleep with, but I definitely wanted to do it before my friends did so I could be really cool and experienced. Plus this guy was a prince! Cute, sensitive, piano-playing college guy? I mean, come on. So anyway, we talked a little and passed out, and he snuck out early the next morning—my parents never found out.

Can you even imagine how amazing this sounded back at high school? My friends were in awe and I was like, "Guys, it doesn't hurt at all," even though I was, like, so in pain. After that, I was on cloud nine. I had junior prom and lost a little bit of weight, and the pianist didn't disappear. We saw each other a few times after, although USC wasn't near where I lived. Still, I hung on to every single moment that we shared. I've been thinking about the whole experience lately because I'm preparing to be a bridesmaid again this summer. I'm looking forward to it, but now it's a totally different ball game—there's nothing nearly as good as your first time.

—C, 27

THE SOLE SINGLETON

I'M FROM MISSISSIPPI, and I'm thirty, so all my friends from home are married. When I say that I have no single friends, I'm not talking single like without boyfriends. I'm saying that I'm the only unmarried one. The last of them got married to her college sweetheart last year. (Vomit.)

For that wedding, the entirely blond bridal party was comprised of my five best sorority sisters from Ole Miss. They all got engaged at the same time about a year earlier, and I expected to get engaged at around that time too. Then I found out that my boyfriend of four years was sleeping with his coworker. I had a bit of a nervous breakdown and moved to Manhattan. The wedding marked my first trip back to Mississippi.

I had been single for only a few months when the bride invited me to her bachelorette party, which wasn't a traditional one but instead a couples' weekend in Charlotte—I was the only single person invited. (I didn't go.) The single-shaming continued at the wedding rehearsal, when I realized that there were four groomsmen and five bridesmaids, and that I was the only singleton in the bunch. I was the self-conscious, unmarried thirty-year-old bridesmaid who had to walk by herself down the aisle. When I found my table at the rehearsal dinner, I saw that I was sitting with three married couples, with an empty seat beside me. We spent the evening talking about diamond clarity in engagement rings, home-improvement projects, and the brand of paint everyone was buying at Lowe's. I cried in the bathroom, drank too much, and had to call my dad to collect me.

The bridesmaids were set to wear shiny praline-colored dresses that had a significant shoulder on one side and a thin spaghetti strap on the other. To me, the idea of a bunch of white girls in skin-colored taffeta was extremely unappealing, but I still called the dress store and had mine shipped to my family home. I knew it would fit because I had already worn three bridesmaid dresses from this store, which was a bridal warehouse in a Biloxi strip mall. So the day of the wedding was the first time I tried on the dress. Jesus, was it unflattering. It was tight, with ruching and a knee-length cut, and it had a big crease in the skirt area from the way it was folded when it was mailed. Turns out I'm not real domestic—no wonder I'm not married, right?—because when I went to iron it out, I burned a quarter-size hole in the crotch of the dress. Since the taffeta was super synthetic, the area around it quickly became warped so that the entire disaster zone was about the size of a tennis ball.

I took a shot of tequila, drove to the chapel, and burst into tears. I showed my dress to my other sorority sisters. We decided I'd hold the bouquet in front of it, and maybe no one would notice. I drank some champagne and some bourbon and got high on hairspray fumes as we got done up. My hair was crazy—teasing, curls, a half-updo, the whole works—but that was the least of my concerns. When I got into the dress, it was clear that the bouquet trick wouldn't work. The wedding planner got wind, pulled me and another bridesmaid into the bathroom at the chapel, and told me to take off the dress. She started sewing the sides of the hole together while I stood beside her, crying quietly, wearing nothing but a thong and a pashmina.

Between her fix and some strategic bouquet-holding, the bride didn't find out about the hole. But while I was getting into the car that would take me to the reception, I ripped apart both the wedding planner's patch-up job and the skinny strap on one shoulder when I lifted my arm too fast. So at this point, I had a bum sleeve and an undies-baring hole in my dress. I was also drunk: We had been locked up in the chapel all day with ample booze and no lunch. So I decided to stand outside the reception and chain-smoke cigarettes. And from there, it gets hazier and hazier in my head.

I hope that my drunken messiness can be explained by how emotional I felt about being newly single—about walking down the aisle in Mississippi for another wedding that wasn't mine. The worst thing I did that night was call my ex-boyfriend's roommate to invite him to meet me at the reception. Thirty minutes later we were making out on the dance floor as my friends pretended not to see. It was completely inappropriate. I looked like Kurt Cobain with my ripped dress, my limp ringlets, and my bangs plastered to the side of my head. The best thing I did that night was decide not to go home with him. Instead, I woke up the next morning on another bridesmaid's couch, still wearing my ripped, holey praline taffeta dress.

I had only been living in New York for a few months, but I couldn't wait to get back to the city after that weekend. The way I look at it, being thirty in New York is like being twenty-fve in Mississippi; I gained a good five years of my life back by making one simple move. Whereas I don't know another single person at home, there are about fifteen single girls in my office in New

York, all of whom are around my age. At first, it was shocking to me. But it's also such a relief. I'm not opposed to being in a relationship, but I'm not even close to shoving anyone down the aisle.

—H, 30

THE EIGHTIES IRISH SHOTGUN BRIDESMAID

THE YEAR WAS 1985. My brother was twenty-two, and he had been dating this girl for two years before he broke it off. They had already planned on going on a holiday with a bunch of friends a few weeks later, though, so they went on the trip and had one last hookup. Two months later, my brother and I were in the kitchen of our family home—which is in Ireland, just outside Galway—and he said he had some news. He took a deep breath and said, "I'm going to be a dad." I jumped up and grabbed the Bible and started looking for baby names—I was nineteen, and this was my idea of humor at the time—but he sat me down again and said that they were going to get married. He wanted me to be a bridesmaid.

My brother and I were very close, but we had seven sisters—and his fiancée had four sisters—so I was surprised to be asked. I was also horrified. I was a tomboy; I did not want to have to get into a fancy dress. I'm one of twelve, and partly because of time constraints, we're not ones to examine our emotions. He didn't have to explain why he wanted me in the wedding; "you're very special to me" and all that. It was more like, "We're getting married. Are you going to be in the wedding or not?"

The bride was twenty years old and two months pregnant

when they found out, so it was very quickly and excitedly arranged. It would be in her town just outside Galway, and I was lucky because I didn't have to do anything to help with the planning; her mother and sisters were all busybodies, so they just told me what to wear and when to turn up. Every woman she knew was invited to her hen party—there were sixty of us there, including her mother and her grandmother—and we went to the local club. She couldn't drink, of course, but that didn't stop her from being ridiculed: We put her into a baby carriage and brought her up the street, stopping every man to make him kiss her.

On the morning of the wedding, I would have loved to stay in my family home while my brother was getting ready. This was partly because we were close, and partly because I had a crush on his best friend, a groomsman. Did I mention I was nineteen? But instead, I headed over to the bride's home to face the dress. I don't know how to describe it—can we just say it was the eighties and leave it at that? It was a big yellow confection with huge, puffy, three-quarter-length sleeves, a bow at the back, and a big crinoline skirt—I don't remember what my shoes were like because I couldn't see them. I looked like a daffodil.

As the hairdresser puffed out my bangs and made my long bob look even more eighties than it already was, I told her that I was a bag of nerves. This was my first time in a wedding, and I was the fourth bridesmaid so I had to go down the aisle first. Plus, I had hooked up with two of the three groomsmen—the best man I hadn't been with, purely because he was my brother—and I was sort of embarrassed about that. So she gave me a shot of whiskey. When she put the baby's breath in my hair, I thought that maybe I looked more like a buttercup than a daffodil, and I knew I needed another shot. I then spent the rest of the time before the wedding trying to slink away from everyone so the videographer wouldn't get me on film.

When my big moment arrived, I didn't do the proper step-step-step; I ran-ran-ran. I could see my brother at the altar making gestures for me to slow down. But I just couldn't! After me came the bride, who everyone knew was pregnant not only because it was impossible to keep a secret in those villages, but also because she was wearing the tightest mermaid dress, which made her bump all the more visible. I liked her, but she was still marrying my favorite brother and I felt like she was taking him away. I have seven sisters and four brothers, and he and I were always the closest; he protected me from my younger brother, who was a monster. That said, I wasn't too emotional. I giggled all the way through the wedding because it took the bride ten minutes to put the ring on my brother—in their haste, they had bought it a size too small.

I can't remember the food at the reception, but I know the speeches were funny—even the priest took a few whiskeys and made some pregnancy jokes that my mom certainly didn't appreciate. When the meal and the speeches were over, there were "the afters," an Irish tradition: A busload of acquaintances arrives and everyone parties until the early morning.

The dress brought back horrible memories of my first communion, and my hair was too feathered for anyone's liking, but it was one of the greatest nights I can remember. There were so many young people filled with so much goodwill toward the couple, and we just danced nonstop until four or five in the morning. Was the bride having a good time? I have no idea. But she did look beautiful, even in her horrendous eighties dress. And when we gave them a big send-off around midnight, I surprised myself by crying—I knew that, despite the circumstances, my brother was properly in love. It was the worst dress I ever wore, but it was the best wedding I ever attended.

—H, 44

THE TWO-TIME BRIDESMAN

MY FRIENDS GOT ME A SHIRT that says ALWAYS A BRIDES-
MAID; NEVER A BRIDE. It's weird because I'm a straight guy. But
I've also been a bridesmaid in two weddings.

The first wedding I was in was my sister's. She wanted a
small, sentimental ceremony, and she asked me to be her maid of
honor. I was like, "Awesome—what the hell does that mean?"
She just wanted me to stand by her side during the wedding,
which was just for immediate family. The priest looked at me
funny, but that was about it.

The second wedding was my friend Charlotte's. We met in
our sixth-grade English class, when I tied her shoes to her desk.
She sat behind me, she fell over, and she thought it was hilarious.
From then on, she was like another sister to me. She dated all my
friends, we watched hockey together, she gave me a puppy from
her dog's litter. And eventually, when we went to college together,
we'd turn to each other for advice on the opposite sex: "What
could I have possibly done wrong?" "Why is he being such a
dick?" One night, we were out with a bunch of friends and everyone started joking around about us hooking up. As we were explaining why this would never happen, she yelled, "You're my
gay best friend!" I vehemently objected to that, and she said,

"Fine. You don't have to be my gay best friend, but you do have to be a bridesmaid in my wedding one day." I said that'd be okay as long as she didn't make me match my purple bridesmaid dress to my high heels. I thought that's what bridesmaids do.

After college, she got engaged to one of our friends from high school. Before we could have the big bridesmaid talk, she called me crying. She was calling the wedding off. They had been dating long distance, and they realized they were looking for different things: She was career focused but he wanted to have a bunch of kids right away.

About six months later, she started dating this guy. The deal was that I had to approve of him before they got married. A year went by and I didn't get to meet him—she was in Chicago, and I was in Florida—and one Saturday I called her up and she squealed, "He proposed!" You know when girls are super giddy and it's almost scary? It was like that. He rented out a famous ice rink (she was still a hockey nerd), and he proposed by the center line. So I listened to the whole thing and I had her put him on the phone. I said, "Congratulations, man. Good work. If you do anything to fuck this up, I'm going to find you and break your fucking kneecaps. Put Charlotte back on." Was I totally serious? Well, no. But I hadn't approved of him yet, and I needed to make sure he knew what was up.

Once the wedding planning started, she asked whether I'd be in the wedding. I paused. "Are you going to make me wear a dress? Because if you ask me to I will, and I guess it'd be fucking hilarious to have a dude in a dress. But I'd rather not." Luckily, she said I'd be wearing a tux.

She invited me to the bachelorette party by mailing me an invitation with a huge penis on it. It was sweet. I respectfully declined.

They were getting married on a lake in Wisconsin, and before the trip I desperately tried to find a date. I didn't want to pay for a random girl to fly there from Florida, so I tried to find a Chicago girl who'd go with me. I e-mailed friends and posted this message on Facebook: "I'm a bridesmaid but I don't want to look gay. I'll hook you up for the weekend!" I got one girl on the phone and tried to win her over with talk of free dinner and booze. She was like, "Yeah, but no."

Since I was dateless, I grew a bright red, corkscrew mustache. I have a kid face and it made me look like a pedophile. First thing Charlotte said when she saw me was, "What the fuck is on your face?" I told her I figured every bridesmaid needed a little flair, and she told me I would shave "that thing" off before I walked down the aisle. I just did it for laughs, and I got many in the week leading up to the wedding. A bunch of their friends had rented a house and we all stayed there together, and I embraced this hokey gay look that went with my bridesmaid persona. If everyone thought I was gay, I was going to go for it. I took the mustache to another level by adding a pair of jorts, or jean shorts, which I wore all week. The groom's parents took us to dinner one night and the mother seemed vaguely appalled.

I walked down the aisle with a guy. By this point, nothing could embarrass me. I had shaved my face though, so I didn't look like a complete asshole. I got some confused looks, and some scowls, and did take a bunch of bridesmaid pictures with the other two girls. The groom made the inevitable "Where's your boyfriend?" cracks. I replied in a low voice: "I'm sleeping with your sister tonight." He didn't like that. I kinda did have my eye on her, and we flirted and hung out, but nothing happened. She wasn't that attractive, to be honest with you.

Nah, it was a fun wedding and she was a nice girl. I wasn't nostalgic or emotional at all, but I'm not the kind of guy who'd ever sit back and reflect on that sort of stuff.

A year after the wedding, Charlotte called, upset, and said she and her husband hadn't had sex in two months. She said the spark was gone. I suggested Victoria's Secret and a good talk, but she called a month later to say that she didn't love him anymore. They were getting divorced. When it happened, I questioned my own relationship. At the wedding, they seemed like such a great match. But my friendship with Charlotte taught me that men and women think so differently, and they have to constantly talk about how they're feeling or things can spin out of control. And by the time I met my fiancée, I like to think I was pretty good at honest communication. I guess sometimes it pays to be one of the girls.

—M, 32

THE AXED BRIDESMAID

MY BEST FRIEND, Lena, married a little twerp. She was in a long-term relationship, and she started seeing this guy Martin on the side. He was a short, chubby, totally cocky guy who didn't seem to care that she had a boyfriend. He was a bit of a bigot—he repeatedly called my gay best friend a fag—but here's what sums him up perfectly: He was sharing a room with his brother in his parents' house in the suburbs at the age of thirty-one, but he spent his money on a brand-new Porsche. What a douche.

She was blown away by his Prince Charming act. It didn't matter if I liked him as long as she was happy, of course. But after they had been dating for about two years, something happened. Me, Lena, Martin, and a few of our other friends spent a long day drinking at a boozy brunch place, and the next day she came over crying, with two black eyes, a broken nose, and bruises up and down her legs. She said that they had been walking home from the concert and he was drunkenly yelling at her about something. Some guys stopped to see if she was all right, and one of them punched Martin in the face. He was furious that she hadn't stood up for him. When they got home, she fuzzily remembered him punching her across the nose and pushing her down the stairs. The next morning, she kicked him out and came over, and said that she couldn't say for sure what had happened because she was so drunk. She thought she'd give him the benefit of the doubt. There was no talking her out of it.

Within a couple of days, they were back together. And within a couple of months, they were engaged. I acted like I was happy for her, but I was not happy about her marrying him at all. And then she started doling out bridesmaid duties. She has this thing about me being single and crazy—I'm thirty, and she wants me to settle down. It's not like I'm out partying all the time, but I definitely have a better time than she does. Just days after the engagement, she e-mailed a list of things for me to practice in the year leading up to the wedding. It had stuff on it like "Make sure to learn how to dance properly so you don't look embarrassing" and "Break in your heels so you don't have to change your shoes at the reception." It was super silly, but she was serious—for the next nine months, she took control of my life in any way she could.

First, I drove an hour and a half to a bridesmaid dress place and sat in the fucking store for two hours while she hemmed and hawed about dresses. I texted for all of two minutes before she snapped, "Get off the phone—this is my day." Otherwise it was pretty uneventful, but a few weeks later, I still didn't have a say in the dresses, and we got these long purple gowns with one strap— they were horrible, and three hundred dollars. Next came no fewer than three showers; attendance at all three was required. She told me she would kill me if I came to any of them hungover. She treated me like a crazy college kid just because I didn't have a boyfriend.

The first shower went okay, and the morning of the second shower I texted her a joke: "I'm hungover—will be late." She texted back, "Get here now." A little while after, I went to a wedding and put pictures on Facebook. I was wearing a beige floral-print dress, and she texted me within seconds of the album going up: "You better not wear white, beige, or cream to any of my wedding events." I felt like I was at her beck and call, and she felt like I wasn't doing enough. "Carol [another bridesmaid] has offered to put gift bags together for the hotel rooms," she texted one day. "You haven't offered to do anything." I felt like I was constantly asking if I could help, but she wouldn't give me anything to do.

By the third shower, which was on a Sunday, I was fed up. I was going to a college football game that weekend three hours from where we lived, and as I planned the trip I had an inkling that I'd be skipping shower number three. The week before I had tested the waters, and she said she'd kill me if I missed it. Still, when I woke up on Sunday morning in the college town, I knew I wasn't going to make it to the shower. I texted her, apologizing, and asked if I could take her to dinner later that week to make up for it. She responded with a torrent of texts: "Get your life together—you're acting like a college student," "Everyone is married and you're still single," "You should have sent a baked good." If you know me you know I would have never sent a baked good.

So we got in a text war and she said she didn't know whether she wanted me to be in the wedding. She said that she was ready for a new chapter in her life, and that I was lagging behind; she thought I didn't have my head on straight. But I wouldn't have treated marriage like she did: Lena was at the age where she felt it was expected of her, and she happened to meet someone, so she just thought he would do. She was judging me, and I was judging her. I called her a few times and she hung up. It was like fighting with a boyfriend.

You remember my gay best friend? He was tipsy that evening, and texted her that she needed to stop being such a bitch. This launched a whole new text war, with all the other bridesmaids joining the fray. I finally stopped responding and wrote an e-mail to Lena on Monday morning, apologizing and saying that I wanted to be there for her on her wedding day. She replied with a four-page e-mail that ended with a real kicker: Leave my bridesmaid dress with the doorman, and Martin would pick it up and leave me a check for the dress price.

I was unbelievably hurt. Without thinking, I sent a mean e-mail back. "You've been the worst bridezilla," "I don't want to be in the wedding anyway"—that sort of thing. She forwarded the message—just my part, not hers—to all the other bridesmaids, and they suddenly stopped talking to me. These girls, including Lena, were like sisters to me. I had known them since kindergarten.

Lena got married the next month. I wasn't even invited to the wedding. I called and texted, and she never replied. Of course her fiancé already hated me, so he was probably pushing her to freeze me out. I miss her friendship—I saw her at a friend's wedding and she didn't speak to me. It was sad. I e-mailed, hoping that I could repair at least some of the damage, and she replied a week later and said she was really busy at work. I don't think we're going to be friends again—I think the e-mail was the end of the story. A few weeks ago, I heard that she was pregnant and my gay friend said they'll have the ugliest kids ever—which is mean but probably true.

The next time I was asked to be a bridesmaid, I made sure I was the best ever. It helped that I felt fully supportive of the marriage. I planned the showers and the bachelorette party, I even helped the bride pick the wedding dress. I would give myself five stars. And I now know that the psycho prewedding person is not really your friend. There's a little bridezilla in everyone—maybe it'll happen to me too.

—N, 31

THE ODD GIRL OUT

I'VE BEEN A BRIDESMAID TEN TIMES, and believe me, it has been insane. I thought the worst would be the one where the theme colors were seemingly inspired by the Easter Bunny's barf. Half of the dozen bridesmaids wore pastel green—the other half wore lavender. All of us looked ridiculous, and the dresses were so poofy that we could hardly fit in the church's aisle.

But things were certainly weirder when I was in the wedding of a semirandom friend from college. We didn't know each other that well: We just spent a ton of time together because we were on the board of a club together, so our friendship was almost professional. This sounds obnoxious, but she thought we were best friends and I thought we were, you know . . . friends. Anyway, her boyfriend proposed when we were twenty-five, and she called to ask if I'd be in the wedding. She was very sweet—almost angelic—and I thought it'd mean something to her if I was in the wedding. Still, I dreaded the commitment of time and money.

She was the sort of girl who never drank, so I was interested to see what her bachelorette weekend would be like. I arrived in Chicago for the weekend and met the eight other bridesmaids, who were friends of hers from high school. They were nice and dorky—exactly what I expected. We played pin-the-penis-on-the-groom and a trivia game about all the guys she hooked up with before her fiancé. We drank pretty heavily, but I think everyone must have been way ahead of me . . . because when we got to a crowded bar in downtown Chicago and I was waiting to order a cocktail, I turned around to find the bride making out with one of her bridesmaids.

It's not like she was a partier. Going out wasn't her thing, let alone making out with other girls. Just imagine happening upon the most innocent girl you know making out with her childhood best friend! I was so surprised that I think I laughed, but when all the other bridesmaids started making out with each other I was seriously shocked and confused. Was this part of my duty as a bridesmaid? The bride and her friends definitely weren't lesbians, so it was clear that this was their last night out in the world for a long time, and they somehow thought this was the craziest thing they could do. When the maid of honor came toward me I freaked out. I don't know whether she was actually going in for a kiss, but she started assuring me that it was no big deal—the bride had done this sort of thing before in high school.

All the bridesmaids had boyfriends, and they all seemed very sensible. It was bizarre. I got drunk and tried to be a good sport while also not making out with anyone. The next morning, I woke up and was like "Oh my god that was effing insane!" No one mentioned it, and then someone brought it up jokingly and it was really uncomfortable.

Anyway, we got our bridesmaid dresses the morning after as well, and mine was three sizes too big and also a terrible Barbie-pink satin. Between that and the night before, I was so freaked out that I took an early flight home.

The wedding itself was boring by comparison. All the bridesmaids had their boyfriends with them, and when I saw some shots being taken at the reception I wondered if they'd repeat their party-girl performances. But there was no bridesmaid-on-bridesmaid action at the wedding, which was probably for the best.

After that, I fell out of touch with the bride. It has been seven years now, and I sometimes think about how it's weird that I'm in the wedding pictures in her apartment. My sister-in-law had eight bridesmaids in her wedding, and she's not friends with half of them anymore. I guess it happens, but it's weird to see these strangers in frames on your wall.

So now that I've put myself in odd situations, and spent lots of time and money on my bride friends, I wonder who I'll have in my own fictional wedding—which is in the distant future since I'm single at the moment. Part of me wants to get payback and say, "All of you bitches have to spend two thousand dollars on me!" But part of me wants to have a lean party because I don't want to deal with any of my friends' drama. In a way, having a wedding party is like bragging about how many friends you have, and I don't think I'll need that as an older bride. And by now I've been to enough bachelorette parties that I've gotten all the partying out of my system. The only thing I can guarantee is that you won't find me flirting with bisexuality in my final days as a single gal.

—P, 32

THE ASTROLOGER

I DON'T UNDERSTAND these people with a lot of bridesmaids. They must have way too much time on their hands! I pulled my wedding together with four children and my sister. I borrowed my neighbor's children because I knew them and I loved them. They were little ballerinas, and I dressed them in beribboned velvet dresses that were a deep rose color. To me, being surrounded by children on my wedding day was the most beautiful thing.

I love weddings. I'm an astrologer, a romantic, and a writer, and I love the dress and the artistic expression of the bride. Plus, weddings are good marker points. They make you think. If you are invited to be in one, it means that the couple loves you enough to want you to mark this major transition with them. It's the most incredible thing to get married and to look at all the people who have wandered into your life. You don't need the piece of paper; you need the experience of walking over a threshold to the next chapter. A wedding changes you. I can't articulate it—it's like explaining what it's like to swim, or to try chocolate pudding for the first time. It's the most amazing experience, so people say, "Why not do it sooner?" But the little seed has to grow, and if you're not ready nothing can make that happen.

There's no rehearsal for life, as they say, and we have certain proclivities that play out during the wedding prep. It's a time when you can learn about yourself. Do you want the reception to be romantic or less so? Private or big? I could never predict how you'll feel at that juncture, especially because the wedding you would plan at eighteen might be different than the one you'd have at thirty-five. Things change and you don't even realize it. That's why these marker points—when you get engaged, get married, have a baby, buy a house—are important. You should think about where you have come from, and where you are now.

If you have a large number of bridesmaids, you are multiplying the chances of some people not getting along. I'm speaking as a person, not an astrologer. I didn't even think of having bridesmaids because I was so inspired by the children I had in my wedding. Their mother was this Frenchwoman who had sacrificed everything for her beautiful daughters. I wanted to be reminded of what this life is about: grace, innocence, and beauty.

My sister didn't pick me to be her matron of honor because we were brought up Catholic, and she married a Jewish man. She felt that I wouldn't understand the traditions of the wedding, so she asked her husband's sister instead. I was still a bridesmaid, though. Her wedding was on the beach under a beautiful tent. It rained the morning of and she was terrified. I was saying Hail Marys and she was crying and saying that the musicians would be electrocuted. But it stopped at just the right time.

My sister met her husband on an eclipse, which, well, could really go either way. I didn't want to read her charts before the wedding because I didn't want to know if it was a bad day. Apparently it was a very good day, because she's been happily married twenty years, and she has two children.

An astrologer should never tell you whether to marry someone. I might read a couple's charts and say, "Have you talked about money? I see she likes spending money," and the guy will laugh and say, "You picked up on that, huh?" which is a good sign. A good marriage isn't about being different from or similar to your partner—it's about liking those differences or similarities. Everyone has that one sticky problem that never gets resolved. If I see a serious problem, like infidelity, then I'll encourage a couple to sort it out immediately. Because once you have kids, you are running a small corporation, and the traits that matter are not the ones you look for when you are dating.

If I talk to an engaged couple who is questioning marriage, I'll tell them to wait for an eclipse. Eclipses bring out latent issues you may not have even thought about before the wedding. Take Kim Kardashian: Before her first wedding, she was on such a track to get married that she wouldn't let anything get in the way. I see that a lot. But I advise couples to let an eclipse stress their partnership to the max. Once the gale-force winds blow through your life and everything flies out the windows, you'll see if you're ready.

And this bridesmaids stuff? You've got to know you love the couple if you're going to commit. My daughter joyfully planned a wedding in Bali as a bridesmaid, which was a learning experience. She was shipping things to an island and dealing with detailed customs stuff. I say if you want to be a bridesmaid, do it—but if you truly don't, don't.

—SUSAN MILLER

THE BRIDEZILLA VICTIM

I'LL BE A BRIDESMAID in my friend Lara's wedding in a few months, which has been a nightmare for me. Not only has she been a bridezilla, but I'm not sure whether I should even be supporting the marriage. She has dated her boyfriend, Jeff, for five years—and she has cheated on him for four of those five.

Lara and I have been friends since we were toddlers. She's like a bad Catholic school girl with a twinkle in her eye. Whenever there's an opportunity for rebellion, she'll take it. Like, she has smoked for years and her very proper mother doesn't know—whenever her mom turns away she lights one up. Sometimes, she doesn't seem to have feelings.

From the moment she started dating Jeff, she was seeing other people even though Jeff thought they were exclusive—it's like she didn't know why she was dating Jeff anymore, but she just kept him around. Two years into it, she had two full-on boyfriends at the same time. She met the other guy at a bar, and he was married. They dated for two years. She would talk to me about the situation, and I'd just beg her to get out of it. She said they were in love, and I do think they were, but she only realized how bad things were when she found out his wife was five months pregnant. She left him, he went crazy on her, and his wife found out about everything. The wife e-mailed Jeff to tell him, but Lara wiggled her way out of it. She said the guy was crazy, and her boyfriend believed her. She's an expert at manipulation.

When Lara told me they were engaged, I was shocked. I just never thought she was in love with Jeff. They're so different. She likes to party; he's really nice and calm. He's into sports; she's not. She loves to travel; he's a homebody. And he would never cheat on her. I thought she kept him on hand because he's a solid guy, but I never thought they'd get married.

I'm the maid of honor, and there are eleven other bridesmaids. The wedding has been constantly dramatic and it hasn't even happened yet. In the nine months since the engagement, I have gotten probably four hundred e-mails from her mom, and I'd say half of them are criticisms of me or negative comments. In the other half, she's nitpicking about details of the bridesmaid dresses, the shower, the bachelorette. The shower invitation alone necessitated dozens of notes, and the finished product was five pages: two leaf inserts and a front and back cover.

The bachelorette has been the biggest bone of contention. The twelve bridesmaids live all over the country—and we're each spending three hundred dollars on our dresses and about two hundred dollars on shower and wedding gifts—so we figured we could afford five hundred dollars each for the bachelorette. I told Lara this and she said she wanted to go to Acapulco. No one could afford it. I e-mailed Lara to tell her, and within five minutes her mom called me. She said Lara was in floods of tears and absolutely devastated. She demanded an explanation. What can you even say to that? I didn't know how to deal.

The next day, Lara called and said she wanted me to present options of destination bachelorette parties we could afford. I did it. I made a spreadsheet of the trips we could do—a friend's time-share in San Diego, a beach house in New Jersey, an apartment in Tampa—and she told me she didn't like anything. She said she'd rather do nothing, which inspired more tears and disappointment.

After that, Lara wrote us an e-mail saying that the most stressful part of her wedding planning has been dealing with the bridesmaids. Her mom wrote shortly after, asking me to explain why the bachelorette was canceled. I ignored the e-mail because I thought she wouldn't like my reply, and she e-mailed twice more within twenty-four hours. So I wrote back. I said the only places we could afford weren't good enough. It was a firm e-mail and Lara told me it really upset her mother. She asked me to apologize. Yeah, right.

I don't think the marriage is going to last. Maybe I'm not being as accommodating as I could be because of that. I don't think she has cheated since they have been engaged, and I do love him—I think he's great. But I'm wary. I think that if you're nitpicking about all these little details, and you have her past, then this might not be right.

I thought about talking to her about whether this is really what she wants, but after all the wedding drama there just hasn't been time. And now I'm happy to say, "You've made your bed, now lie in it." I don't even know if we'll be friends after the wedding. I'm definitely walking on eggshells with her mom. The wedding is in three months, so I have time to see what happens.

—T, 33

THE BACKCOUNTRY BRIDESMAID

I MET THE BRIDE when we were in Honors English class at age fourteen. She had spent most of the semester carving "Frodo Lives" into her desk and wearing a feathered cap. I thought she was strange. But we were in six classes together, and one day I saw her eyeing another freshman in the back of the room. I marched up to her and said, "You've got a crush on that guy! What's the deal?" She blushed, and blinked, and was like, "How did you know?"

Alison and I were unlikely friends for the rest of high school, and she always dished about the guys in her life and offered her perspective on my boyfriends—whether I wanted to hear it or not. When we went to college, she met her dream man. He was a great guy with shoulder-length hair and a knack for working with computers. She was an aspiring reenactor of colonial scenes with a passion for historical archiving. They both loved historical reenactments, *The X-Files,* and archive research. When we were twenty-three, I went with them to a chess tournament and she said, "Oh, yeah—I'm engaged. Will you be my maid of honor?"

Her fiancé was from Arkansas, and her grandparents had lived in a tiny town there too. I drove to the wedding, and the town was so backcountry that it wasn't on the map. This was 2011, when the rapture was supposed to happen, so there were all of these hand-lettered signs on the side of the very desolate road: "Prepare for the rapture," "Jesus is coming for you." I drove and drove, and eventually arrived in the town, which wasn't really a town but a series of big farms.

I stayed in a motel on the outskirts, and the next morning I met Alison at her house. She normally wears men's clothes: button-down shirts, corduroys, that sort of thing. So she looked really pretty in her black wedding dress—she had gotten it on sale at Macy's. She was pottering around and tidying up, and her dad came in and said she needed to shovel this dead possum off the road. She said, "No, man—it adds to the ambience," but then laughed, grabbed a shovel, and marched outside in her wedding dress and little heels. Just like that, she scooped up the roadkill and tossed it into the weeds.

Alison gave me a mason jar of moonshine for my bridesmaid's gift, and the reception was a pig roast with a bluegrass band. The food was great and the dancing was fun. I had met some of the groomsmen beforehand—one wore an animal paw on a leather cord around his neck—and I knew some other people as well, so I wasn't totally out of my element.

Alison and I are certainly unlikely friends. I'm your typical young professional, and I don't think I'd be brave enough to shovel up roadkill in my wedding dress. But we go way back. We got closer when my dad died after I graduated from high school. My neighbor wrote a poem about him and I asked Alison to write it in calligraphy so I could give it to my mom. We worked on the project together, and she did a beautiful job. I felt like I was returning the favor by being in her wedding. I love seeing how much her husband adores her, and I was honored and flattered to be part of their day.

After the wedding, the bridal party went back to my motel room and I started talking to one of the groomsmen. He and his wife seemed pretty nice. He asked if I was dating anyone, I said no, and he said, "Well, if you're interested in me . . ." I said, "You're married!" and he said something along the lines of: "Yeah, my wife and I were talking about asking you to have some fun with us." So, yes, I was propositioned to have a threesome in small-town Arkansas. I declined and peered at the wife, who was innocently engrossed in discussion with people across the room. He said I knew where to find him if I changed my mind.

—K, 26

THE DRUNK BRIDE'S BRIDESMAID

I DON'T EVEN KNOW if Sylvie remembers the speech I gave at her rehearsal dinner. I thought it was good—heartfelt and funny—but when I looked at her she wasn't paying the slightest bit of attention. She was either looking down or to the side. She was wasted. If I were the bride, I would have been more appreciative and more emotional—I mean, my speech was pretty nice. But I wasn't too upset about her reaction, because she didn't seem to comprehend a thing.

Her speech followed mine, and she talked about the most random stuff. But mainly puppies and lawn mowers. The love-for-lawn-mowers tangent lasted at least two minutes. She did thank her in-laws and her parents, but she also kept sporadically bursting into leg-slapping laughter. Literally, she was doubled over laughing and slapping her leg. It was a riot, but her parents and in-laws were obviously horrified. Everyone was looking between the in-laws and the bride, and although they made an effort to laugh, it was clear they were frightened. Sylvie's fiancé seemed to think it was pure comedy, but he snuck her out over his shoulder once the speeches were through.

Sylvie and I have known each other since grade school. I guess I'm her oldest friend, but I thought it was random of her to ask me to be her maid of honor since we didn't really speak for a few years leading up to the wedding. I didn't hang out with her much in college, but it appeared that she'd learned to party hard. Once she named me her maid of honor, we talked a lot on the phone as I planned her bridal shower and her bachelorette party, and I made sure she was all set for the wedding. Funnily enough, the bachelorette party was pretty tame: We went to Palm Springs and went out dancing, but there were no significant shenanigans to report.

The morning after the rehearsal dinner, there was no mention of the night before. But there was more drinking. Sylvie drank champagne throughout the day, and she hardly ate. She had lost like fifteen pounds leading up to the wedding, and between that, the hangover, the photographer's flashes, and the excitement of the big day, she was feeling pretty loose. The wedding was in the beautiful Catholic church we had grown up going to every Sunday, and I guess it was a little warm. So at the point in the ceremony when they were about to exchange rings, you could see that she was going to fall over. I was standing right behind her at the altar, so I mouthed to the groom to catch her. He caught her in his arms and I screamed for a doctor.

The faces in the audience were aghast. People didn't think she had died or anything, but they were definitely worried. Her dad appeared to be more concerned than her mom. Someone got a cold towel on her forehead and she quickly responded, raising her hand so that the congregation could see she was okay. But she was still down for a good ten minutes. It felt like forever. Finally, she got up and finished the ceremony. She seemed a little embarrassed, but she played it off okay and the rest of the night was fine; she ate, she danced.

Since we weren't that close before the wedding, it wasn't weird that we lost touch after the event. I saw her at a mutual friend's wedding and she was acting rude. She talked loudly during the speeches and reception, saying things like "If I was the bride I would have kicked that bitch out of the wedding" and "Wow, nice to see that our table is all the way in the kitchen." It was embarrassing, and it was even worse when a friend of the groom's parents came up to us and said, "What is your friend doing?" I can't say what he saw her doing, but she was wearing a tiny dress so that you could literally see up her butt when she was dancing. So maybe this guy took that the wrong way—who knows? Again, her husband didn't seem to mind. They're both quirky, and they can be unaware of their surroundings, so he didn't notice anything was wrong.

After that, I thought we were in different places in our lives. Sylvie is a unique person, and I still like her, but we have drifted apart. I'm so glad she is happy in her life. But after that second wedding I realized she had defriended me on Facebook—no idea why. Unfortunately, whenever I get engaged, I think I'll have to invite her to my wedding because our moms are friendly. I can't wait to see what she wears.

—E, 27

THE DRUNK BRIDESMAID

NATALIE WAS READY to be a housewife at age thirteen. She's from Tennessee, and we went to college together up north. When she moved into the dorm she had an entire box filled with pink sweaters. Her freshman-year dorm room was filled with pink signs that said things like STOP AND LOVE LIFE and SHOES ARE A GIRL'S BEST FRIEND. I thought I would hate her, but I ended up loving her. She's the best friend you could ask for. She's fun, she's a great cook, she's outgoing and friendly, and she has a good time no matter what she's doing.

Doug is basically her opposite. He's the kind of kid who sits in cargo pants and watches football while drinking Miller Lite. She was his first girlfriend. Sophomore year, she decided she loved him. He had zero interest in her, but she was relentless. We went out almost every night sophomore year, and almost every night she would knock on his dorm-room door until he answered and let her in. The only reason they're together is because she'd bring him over to our house and feed him chicken and steaks and give him beer. He would do nothing—just sit there and not even contribute to the conversation.

She wanted to be engaged since the day they graduated college, but he moves like molasses. Every time they'd go to her parents' house, the first thing her mom would say was, "When are you getting engaged?" Every Thursday, Natalie would call me and say, "I think we're going to get engaged this weekend! I'm so excited—I can feel it." And on Monday she'd call again, so pissed that he hadn't proposed. For six months before they got engaged, she checked his bank account every day to see if he had bought the ring. He called when he was at the ring store to make sure she definitely wanted to do this. At the engagement party, her mom said, "At least he looks somewhat happy."

When they did get engaged, Natalie was really happy. The only thing I said to her is, "You're a giver, and I want to make sure you're in a relationship with someone who gives back." He doesn't give much at all in my opinion, but if she's happy, she's happy. I hope it works out.

The rehearsal dinner. I would describe it as awkward. I didn't give a speech, but the rest of the nine bridesmaids all got up with tears in their eyes and spoke to accompanying slideshows. As I said, Natalie is the best friend. She's the kind of friend who brings you soup when you're sick and makes you feel like a queen on your birthday. So all nine speeches were heartfelt and amazing. Then there was only one speech on his side, from his best man. And even that was about how great Natalie is. I was sweating I was so uncomfortable. I wanted to stand up and say, "I love you, Doug! It might seem like no one cares, but we do!"

The wedding was at a lodge by a lake in the mountains. Natalie's mom got her hair done and she didn't like it at all. She stood up and started ripping the bobby pins from her hair and throwing them all over the room while yelling, "I fucking hate my hair! I hate it!" She cried, Natalie cried, Natalie's sister cried. The mom stormed out and another friend ran into her in the hallway and said, "Hi, Mrs. Lawrence, is there anything I can do to help?" The mom said, "You can cut off my fucking hair."

She has always been terrifying, so this wasn't totally surprising. And it wasn't like we had a minute until we had to leave. She had like three hours to wash and blow-dry her hair.

That was about all the action until I had too much to drink at the reception. It's just that weddings are so exciting! It's great to be around all these people you never get to see. I get overstimulated and overexcited, and this is how I respond. All of a sudden I was in the hotel room of this strange, cute guy, and he was mashing up Adderall for me to snort. He ended up hooking up with another one of the bridesmaids. It was too bad because he was really cute.

My strapless pink chiffon dress was too big, so every time I raised my arms on the dance floor my boobs would pop out. I thought it was hilarious. I started acting crazy, rolling around on the dance floor and inadvertently flashing people. I was lying on my back and kicking my legs, and no one stopped me. Natalie just laughed about it. She always says, "Oh, you," whenever I act like that.

Later that night, I went skinny-dipping with a couple and another guy, Mike. We jumped off the dock and splashed around in the water, but when it came time to get out I couldn't find the strength to get back on the dock. Mike had to fish me out, and the maid of honor's fiancé came down to the dock just as I was being lifted onto it like a whale. He literally had a boombox on his shoulder. He looked at me and said, "Nice boobs," and turned and walked away.

I went to college with Mike, and I never thought about hooking up with him. The thought never even flickered into my brain. But that night I wanted to do it. So I went back to the room I was sharing with two girlfriends. One girl was already asleep, and the other took her boyfriend into the closet, where they started having sex. The girl in the bed wasn't asleep for long. I went onto the room's deck with Mike, and, according to her, I said things like "I'm not a slut—I'm not making out with you," and then we'd make out. Then: "I'm not a slut—I'm not going to have sex with you," and then she'd hear us doing just that. The next morning, she was really pissed. Will there be a romance with Mike? Ew, no. I haven't thought about him for a second since the wedding. He has a thick neck that I don't like at all.

The next morning, everyone came into our room to rehash the funniest parts of the night, most of which involved me rolling around topless. Luckily I've been drunk at many a wedding, so it didn't really faze me.

—O, 27

THE BRIDESMAID-IN-WAITING

WHEN YOU GET ASKED to be a bridesmaid, you usually don't doubt that the wedding will actually happen. Especially once you've bought the heinous bridesmaid dress. But that's what happened to me.

Tom was a good friend from growing up, and when he got engaged to Rachel I was excited for them. At first. She asked me to be a bridesmaid and I happily obliged. But they didn't live in the same state—he was in grad school at the time—and they were engaged for two years before they even started planning the wedding.

Tom had a not-quite-girlfriend on the side. He would never have called her a girlfriend, but she was certainly a friend with benefits. He met her at school, and he was obsessed with her—totally head over heels. He'd do everything for her, and one day she was like, "Fine, I guess you can hook up with me." He said they had this "thing." This connection. Considering that, I obviously didn't think he should get married. But he argued that he still loved his fiancée, and that the other girl was a fling. There was no real logic to it, believe it or not.

Deep down, I think they both knew the wedding wasn't happening. But they still went through with planning all the details.

She made us buy these hideous dresses in the ugliest red color from David's Bridal. We ordered them six months before the wedding, and by the time we had gotten them it was off. I can't remember the final straw—the thing that made them cancel the wedding. But neither of them was happy. I think she might have suspected something about him and the girl, but she never confirmed that he had cheated on her. So at least there's that.

I was sad about the breakup. Even if he was the cause of it, it was still hard for him. He clearly called off the wedding with the other girl in mind. He wanted to marry her. But that was never going to happen—she was never that into it, and she didn't want anything to do with him when he was single. What a waste. But it all worked out for the best, because clearly Tom and Rachel weren't meant to be.

Rachel got engaged about two years after they broke up. That devastated him, obviously, because he wanted to be the first. He checked out the ring to see how it compared to his, and I think it made him knuckle down and take stock of his life.

Now, I kind of find it funny. I keep the save-the-date on my fridge as a joke. But I'm also furious that I bought this fucking awful dress that I'll never wear. I couldn't return it because I had taken off the tag, so now it's floating around my parents' house like a rusty old rag. The funny thing is that Tom swears that when he does get married, I'll wear the dress. And you know what, I *will*. Even if it doesn't fit and I have to tape it on, I'll make use of my $150.

—J, 27

THE BUTCH BRIDESMAID

I'VE ALWAYS HATED DRESSES. I've always felt really uncomfortable wearing them, but it wasn't always connected to my sexual orientation. When I came out as a lesbian, all of a sudden it made sense: I wasn't a defective woman, but I was a different kind of woman that I never knew existed.

Butch, to me, means a woman who dresses in a masculine way. Maybe she's identified as a lesbian, maybe she gets called sir sometimes. I don't get mad when people mistake me for a guy, but I don't want them to think I'm a guy. I want them to think I'm a woman who looks good in the clothes that I'm wearing, even though they're men's clothes. (I blog about this kind of stuff at butchwonders.com.)

Gender roles and fashion are so deeply embedded in our minds that people don't question their assumptions about what others should wear. When I came out to my mom, she was okay. Then after a couple of months she said, "I understand that you're a lesbian, but do you have to *look* like one?" That was almost more hurtful than coming out. I tried to have her imagine how she'd feel if she was forced to wear men's clothes for her whole life, and then she was finally allowed to wear a dress. It was exhilarating for me; I felt comfortable at last.

The first time I was a bridesmaid, I still thought I was straight. I had to wear a dress, and I hated it. But first I had to wear heels to the rehearsal, and as we milled around a yard in the early evening, they were like croquet stakes in the grass. I couldn't figure out how the other women weren't sinking into the ground. No one understood; they thought I was crazy. The dress was purple and sleeveless. I'm about five foot eight and 180 pounds, so I'm a big gal. It was fairly low cut, and fairly short. I felt like I was dressed up as a prostitute. I was pissed I had to buy the dress, because—as much as any bridesmaid can say this—I *definitely* wouldn't be wearing it again.

Once we got into the church, the minister did this whole spiel about how the husband is the head of the household and the wife shall obey. I thought he was joking, so I chortled audibly. But he wasn't. The only one who got it was my mother, who also got that I had embarrassed the family. And then, since I couldn't leave well enough alone, I pulled the bride aside and said, "You know, you don't have to agree to all of this stuff." She thought about it, and she approached the minister later that night. It was a whole debacle, and it was basically my fault. The next day, I noticed that the word "obey" had been taken out of his speech.

The next time I was a bridesmaid, I was out. Coming out as a lesbian gives you this wild card to play—it could get me out of anything. I didn't have to get my nails done, I didn't have to get my hair done, I didn't have to wear the dress. Straight girls can't just say, "That's not part of my identity." But now I could. My engaged friend said, "Now that you're out, do you feel comfortable wearing a dress?" I was so glad she asked. I had been dreading the wedding for exactly that reason, but I didn't have the courage to bring it up at that time. It was really insightful of her.

She said I could wear whatever I wanted. The bridesmaids wore light blue dresses; the groomsmen wore black suits and light blue ties. I only had a women's suit—but it was one of those conservative Jones New York androgynous cuts—and I wore it with men's shoes and the tie. It was my first time at a nonlesbian event wearing a tie, and I loved it. In fact, I learned how to tie a tie that day. And I finally understood why people think it's fun to buy new clothes.

But I was nervous. Boy, was I nervous. The people in the room ranged in age from about five to ninety, and ranged in political orientation from super conservative to really liberal. I walked down the aisle with this Hare Krishna guy who refused to wear anything but his bright orange robe, and he was even more out of place than I was. But you know, no one cared about either of us. Maybe they talked about me behind my back, but I don't think so. People said, "You look so nice" or "You look really dapper." We worry about offending the older generation, but my god can they adapt!

It was such a good first experience dressing butch in a big public forum. Since then, I've accumulated so much knowledge that my straight guy friends now come to me for fashion advice. And I was really touched that the bride, in her hectic bridal moment, would stop to think about me and what might make me comfortable. She's not perfect: She asked me to read a poem on the morning of the wedding, explaining that it was too late for me to say no. I was like, "You're a bitch, but of course." We remain very close friends.

—J, 32

THE HOUSE PARTIER

WHEN I WAS AT HARVARD, I lived with ten girls in what we called the Slanted House. It might sound like a sorority, but it wasn't like that. The women in the house were cultish and close-knit, but we thought of ourselves as so feminist and empowered that we would never have joined a sorority.

Jessica was the first to get engaged, and she asked two of our housemates to be bridesmaids. She sent letters to the rest of us. Mine was long and sweet, printed on blue paper and tied with a sparkly ribbon. She wrote about celebrating love and friendship, and she asked whether I'd be part of her "house party." I thought, "Okay, this is exciting, but really what it means is that I'm a secondary bridesmaid." The seven of us laughed about being the B Team, or the JV bridesmaids. We thought it was sweet of her to include us, but funny to give us a fake, honorary title.

Jessica is a curator at a major New York City art museum, and she has incredible taste and an impeccable eye. She is so hip that she did roller derby before everyone else; she introduced us to the high-waisted belt before it was cool. But she's also from the Midwest, so she's traditional. It was an interesting combination to see as the wedding unfolded. With its dual personality, New Orleans was the perfect backdrop: It's artsy and creative, but also really romantic with all the Spanish moss and the beautiful old church where she got married.

When Jessica sent us an e-mail explaining what we should wear, instead of just saying "jewel tones" she wrote about mustard yellows, dusty greens, and deep azures evocative of still lifes from the Dutch Golden Age. She even attached pictures of a few paintings to inspire our dress choices. They depicted fruit on tables in front of green backgrounds. It was funny, but the wedding palate was crystal clear.

I found a really beautiful Erdem dress on sale at a Brooklyn boutique, and I apprehensively sought approval: Would it live up to the curator's vision? It was such a big deal, and you could tell that the colors were meant to tell a story. And they totally did. At the wedding, everything from the flower arrangements to the house party dresses to the framed pictures on the walls of the venue came together like one big work of art.

The house party didn't get ready in the bridal suite, but Jessica did ask us to stop by so she could give us these corsages she made out of fabric. They were perfect and Dutch Master–inspired, of course, and we wore them to denote our house party status. At the church, these two round Southern ladies who ran the show were like, "House party! Get over here" and "Hey, house party, what you standin' around for?" I was like, "Huh? They can't be using Jessica's weird lingo." That was when I finally understood that this was something people see all the time at weddings in the South. Aha! The house party's role was to help the bride with her hosting duties: greet people, hand out programs, help guests find seats, make sure everyone got a drink at cocktail hour, and get the party started on the dance floor.

Of course, none of us had known what a house party was: We were a bunch of East Coast liberals at our first Southern wedding. But I loved the idea. I would much rather have a house party than have bridesmaids—why don't we do this in the North? Weddings are such an intimate look into someone's life—their family drama, their different social groups—and they're so earnest and real that it must be scary for the couple. It's helpful to have friends who'll channel the bride, ease the blending of social groups, and make sure everyone has fun.

For me, being in the house party was a way to support the bride without the stress and obligation that comes with being a bridesmaid. It's like being an aunt: You can help out, but you don't have to deal with anything really annoying. You don't have to plan a fucking awesome bachelorette party, write weekly e-mails checking in on the bride, host a shower, learn up on the bride's and groom's family dynamics, or spend a ton of money. And for the bride, it was a nice way for her to honor us without having a long line of bridesmaids.

We knew Jessica put a lot of time into her wedding, but I don't think any of us imagined the level of detail that we witnessed on the wedding day: An artist friend had created a piece of painted wood that everyone signed; Jessica used tin to make four room-size sunflowers that looked like an art installation and also served as the backdrop for the band; people's table assignments were pinned to vintage handkerchiefs, which we later swung over our heads during a traditional New Orleans dance; the straws in the Pimms Cups had little notes on them from the couple.

Those special details got Jessica into some major wedding magazines, and they also made for easy conversation starters with the granny I met at the cocktail hour and the aunt I sat next to on the bus from the church. And from the moment the Zydeco band started playing—with their washboards, accordions, and

Cajun fiddles—I don't think anyone, old or young, sat down for the rest of the night. At the end of it, we were so glad Jessica went first. No one else has gotten married yet, but we'll know exactly who to turn to when we do.

—C, 28

ACKNOWLEDGMENTS

Mainly, I want to thank the bridesmaids for sharing their stories with me. You guys were thoughtful, honest, funny, crazy, and cool, and you made this project fascinating and fun.

Thanks to Hanya, the most brilliant mentor, for helping me get my book contract . . . and for teaching me about everything (including feminism, writing, and how not to cry), goading my enthusiasm, and frequently commenting on the cleanliness of my hair.

To Stephen and Elizabeth at Picador: Thanks for your patience (which I'm sure I tried), your encouragement, and your fantastic guidance. This has been a thrill thanks in large part to you.

Eileen, sorry I turned your wedding into a publicity stunt! Dermot, Mom, and Dad, thanks for always teaching me and supporting me. You would all make great bridesmaids and bridesmen—and that's my highest compliment.

So many friends got me in touch with bridesmaids, inspired story ideas, or offered advice. I can't thank each of you by name, but here are a few: Stacy, Camilla, Kurt, Merritt, Dan, Alex, Jen, Anna, Lexi, Alison, Maggie and Joe, Micaela, Ben, Kate

M., Kate P. and John, Ali, Mike, Carly, Jackie, Danielle, Marion and Val, Andrew, Meghana, Jake, Sarah S., and Erin.

Finally, thanks to the friends I've made at *Condé Nast Traveler*, to the Simpson Street gals, and to Will.

[8]